MIDLOTHIAN
PUBLIC LIBRARY

Borderland

Borderland
A Midwest Journal

Richard Quinney

The University of Wisconsin Press

The University of Wisconsin Press
1930 Monroe Street
Madison, Wisconsin 53711

www.wisc.edu/wisconsinpress/

Henrietta Street
London WC2E 8LU, England

1   3   5   4   2

Printed in Canada

Library of Congress Cataloging-in-Publication Data

Quinney, Richard.
    Borderland: a Midwest journal /
Richard Quinney.
        pp.   cm.
    Includes bibliographical references.
    ISBN 0-299-17430-1 (alk. paper)
    1. Quinney, Richard. 2. Middle West—Biography.
    3. Middle West—Description and travel. 4. Sociologists—United
States—Biography. I. Title.
    CT275.Q554 A3   2001
    977.03 092—dc21   2001000713

977.03

What is it all about, anyhow, this life of ours? Certainly to be forever weary and worried, to be endlessly soiled with thankless labor and to grow old before one's time soured and disappointed, is not the whole destiny of man!

Hamlin Garland, *A Son of the Middle Border*

The wild things that live on my farm are reluctant to tell me, in so many words, how much of my township is included within their daily or nightly beat. I am curious about this, for it gives me the ratio between the size of their universe and the size of mine, and it conveniently begs the much more important question, who is the more thoroughly acquainted with the world in which he lives?

Aldo Leopold, *A Sand County Almanac*

Contents

Photographs   ix

Preface   xiii

Evening Under Lamplight   1

The Gathering of Fragments   49

A Borderland Almanac   99

Bibliography   185

Photographs

The Quinney Farm, Walworth County, Wisconsin, 1920s   5

W. V. B. Holloway and Lorena Taylor Holloway, May 7, 1916   7

Floyd Quinney and Alice Marie Holloway, Wedding, September 15, 1930   10

Earl Richard Quinney, First Birthday, May 16, 1935   13

A Sunday Afternoon, 1937   15

Working in the Grain Field, 1942   17

Dunham School, Halloween, 1946   19

Pig House, Near Sharon, 1952   21

Students' Observatory, University of Wisconsin, 1957   25

East River, Manhattan, 1969   28

The Farmhouse Basement, November 1969   31

Laura and Anne Quinney, November 1970   34

Chapel Hill, North Carolina, 1974   36

Providence, Rhode Island, 1975   39

South Third Street, DeKalb, Illinois, 1985   41

Stavanger, Norway, 1996   44

Daniel at the Farm, May 1997   46

View of DeKalb, May 1997   48

Backyard, Rolfe Road   83

Elva, DeKalb County   84

Poplar Grove, Boone County   85

The Farm in May   86

Photographs

Muskrat Pond on the Farm	87
Wiring to the Chicken House	88
Old Barn on the Holloway Farm, North of Millard	89
Cherry Valley Road	90
Highway X, West of Allens Grove	91
Central Park, New York	92
Île de la Cité, Paris	93
Kitchen Window, Rue du Plâtre	94
Residence of Albert Camus, Rue Madame	95
Machine Shed on the Farm	96
Annie Glidden Road, North of DeKalb	97
At the End of Rolfe Road	98
Buddha Shrine at the New Hotel Crystal, Pokhara, Nepal	106
Streets of Pokhara	107
Bird Nest in Winter, Rolfe Road	108
Along the Tracks of the Burlington Northern Railroad, Waterman	112
Abandoned Farm, Keslinger Road	113
Tree Grove in a Field of Corn Stubble, Keslinger Road	114
Still Life, Rolfe Road	119
East Lagoon in Winter, DeKalb	120
Kishwaukee River	121
Bedroom, Rolfe Road	127
Balcony View, Rue du Plâtre	128
Abandoned Farm with Jet Trail, Old State Road	129
House at the Farm	141
Dining-room Window with Plants	142
Bedroom	143

Photographs

Crop Duster, Annie Glidden Road   148

Guest Room, Rue du Plâtre   149

Flâneur, Galerie Vivienne   150

The Marsh on the Farm   154

Illinois Central Tracks at Annie Glidden Road   155

Grain Elevator, Highway 64 and Five Points Road   156

Barn Interior   159

Granary   160

Front Porch   161

On Waterman Road   164

Corn Harvest, Highway 30 Overpass   165

Shabbona Lake   166

House in Ruins, Irene Road   170

Grain Elevator and Village Pizza, Malta   171

Reguliersgracht, Amsterdam   172

Tree Trunk and Fungi, Ellwood House   176

Back Bedroom   177

Tracks in Sky and Snow, Annie Glidden Road   178

Elm and Mulberry, Ellwood House   182

Chief Shabbona Forest Preserve   183

Grove of White Pines, DeKalb   184

Preface

How many times have I left the Midwest—and returned—with the words of another midwesterner playing in my ears? The words come to me immediately upon leaving the runway at O'Hare and come to me again when circling for the landing. The words are the opening lines of Charles Lindbergh's *The Spirit of St. Louis.*

> Night already shadows the eastern sky. To my left, low on the horizon, a thin line of cloud is drawing on its evening sheath of black. A moment ago, it was burning red and gold. I look down over the side of my cockpit at the farm lands of central Illinois. Wheat shocks are gone from the fields. Close, parallel lines of the seeder, across a harrowed strip, show where winter planting has begun. A threshing crew on the farm below is quitting work for thc day. Several men look up and wave as my mail plane roars overhead. Trees and buildings and stacks of grain stand shadowless in the diffused light of evening. In a few minutes it will be dark, and I'm still south of Peoria.

We sons and daughters of the middle border—between east and west, north and south—inhabit a special place on a vast continent. No matter how high we fly or how far we travel, we are never far removed from the borderland. I imagine other places in the world where I might live. Places with mountains and oceans, places of international commerce, places that would seem to be at the center of the universe. New York City, for example, or Paris or London. But here I am, product and parcel of the Midwest. I inhabit a land that is as much mental and spiritual as it is geographical. Even when I have left to live in other places, I have always returned out of need to the place that I call home.

How does one live on the border, on the edge of things, and especially, how does one live in this place near the end of one's time? Surely one comes to realize the transience of all things, human and otherwise. A space in a vast and unknowable universe, it takes a certain courage to live a life on the borderland, to attend both to the suffering and the joy of living each day. Solace comes in knowing the wonder of being alive. There is no retirement here, for one follows the passions that hold a life together, that give it meaning. In my case, writing, photography, a sense of place, and family—all affirm this existence as I know and experience it. One finally transcends boundaries and goes beyond the borderland.

There are times when I sense the eternal life, at least the eternal as defined by Wittgenstein: "If we take eternity to mean not infinite temporal duration, but timelessness, the eternal life belongs to those who live in the present." I have sensed the sublime of the eternal—the sublime in everyday life—as I have taken to the road to photograph the landscape of the Midwest and afterward returned home. My spiritual practice has been and continues to be in the daily attention I give to creating a life moment by moment. Earth and sky are joined; I become one with the universe. Experiencing the sublime in everyday life is in the long tradition of the romantic poets, transcendental writers, landscape painters, and all who would be close to the true nature of existence. No other prayer or meditation is needed: grace is everywhere.

Each new year brings the possibility of new life. There is the inevitability of aging, but in aging are opportunities for understanding the reality of our existence. In a diary entry, Anaïs Nin writes: "There are few human beings who receive the truth complete and staggering, by instant illumination. Most of them acquire it fragment by fragment, on a small scale, by successive developments, cellularly, like a laborious mosaic." Only the fragments—but the fragments are everything.

I round out this borderland tale still living on the border. In the stillness of my life, I gather the fragments for another year, a year that marks the passing of the twentieth century. We of the Midwest have been inspired for half a century by Aldo Leopold's *A Sand County Almanac*. The almanac is an homage—month by month—to the life cycle of a Midwest year. At century's end, I make my tribute to another year.

Preface

I continue to make my way across the borderland. A photograph now and then. A few careful words to the day. Always the wonder of existence.

I would like to acknowledge the help of those who have made the writing and completion of this book possible. I want to thank the readers of the manuscript—Norman Denzin, Derek Phillips, and Thom Tammaro—for their comments and suggestions. I am grateful to Paul Clark for printing my photographs and to Steve Delchamps for editorial assistance. I want to acknowledge the work and care given to the book at the University of Wisconsin Press. I am thankful, of course, for the daily support of my family and for the parts they have played in these borderland tales.

Evening Under Lamplight

The world becomes stranger as we grow older. We start from home, wander for a while, and arrive at a place that is more complicated than any we have ever known. Our explorations necessarily intensify as we grow older, but I am heartened by the last line of T. S. Eliot's "East Coker": "In my end is my beginning," a time, Eliot notes, "for the evening under starlight." It is the time one spends with the photograph album, under lamplight.

> There is a time for the evening under starlight,
> A time for the evening under lamplight
> (The evening with the photograph album).
> Love is most nearly itself
> When here and now cease to matter.

I view and study the photographs I have accumulated over a lifetime, passed to me from ancestors, and the photographs I have taken over the last fifty years and more. A lifetime is recounted and enhanced as one moves intensely into a deeper communion. I am transported by photographs under lamplight.

1

A long time ago, on a summer's day, the one who would be my father walked with a camera in his hand across a field that sloped eastward from the barn. He had recently returned to the farm after a six-month trip to California in the fall and winter of 1924–25. He was back now, with new eyes, ready for the long haul. The place of his birth held all the mystery in the world needed for the rest of his life.

Sleek black horses grazed on the hillside. Later the heavier horses of mixed breed would come to work the land. But on this day, the black horses his own father had bought and trained grazed in the sunlight. The love of horses was carried in Irish blood.

The man with the camera that day met the woman of his life at a dance in Delavan on a Saturday night in the fall of 1929. They were married the next September. I was born on a day in May of 1934, and my brother followed in June of 1936. A family was now rooted on the farm in Sugar Creek Township, Walworth County, Wisconsin, on planet earth spinning around a sun in the galaxy Milky Way.

At the end of the field, on the hill sloping to the pond, is the original homestead. The land had been purchased in 1868 by my great-grandparents, John and Bridget Quinney. There are photographs in the aging black albums of life at "the old place." In one, Bridget, sitting in a chair beside the lilac bush, is holding a clay pipe. Her daughter, my great-aunt Kate, and my father's sister Marjorie are standing against the horizon in fine fur hats. My father, age three or four, is dressed in a skirt and a ruffled blouse, following the Irish custom, and posed at the end of the path. His mother, Hattie, would die of consumption the next year.

As young people, Bridget O'Keefe and John Quinney had emigrated from County Kilkenny to escape the potato famine of the 1840s. They married and lived in Yonkers for several years and then made the trek to Wisconsin to join other Irish families in Sugar Creek Township. Their gravestones are eroding in the Catholic section of Spring Grove Cemetery in Delavan. The Celtic-cross relief is barely visible and the engraved words have vanished.

Others had inhabited the land before the Europeans came. The Potawatomi had summered on the oak knoll along the edge of the marsh. They had fished in the creek that flowed through the marsh and they had hunted in the surrounding woods. My father told me that Bridget remembered seeing a family of Potawatomi walking along the ridge south of the house, looking

The Quinney Farm, Walworth County, Wisconsin, 1920s

at the place that had once been their home. Each spring I looked for arrowheads in the plowed fields.

The horses in the photograph are grazing in the field after days of summer work. In the heat of the day, they had pulled the wagons of bundled oats through the fields and up to the threshing machine. The straw blown from the thresher is piled high south of the barn. In another month, the horses will be harnessed for the pulling of wagons stacked with corn. The silo will be filled for the winter supply of silage to feed the milking cows. Some years later, I forked fermenting and moldering fodder down the dark chute each winter night.

Eventually the tractor would replace the horses. The combine would replace the binder and the threshing machine. The remaining horses would be sent to the mink ranch. I would leave the farm, but the farm would never leave me.

2

With a coupon clipped from a box of cereal, my mother ordered a camera. The year was 1916, and the camera arrived on the 25th of March. I know these facts because they are written in a diary that my mother kept at the time. Alice Marie, the only child of W. V. B. Holloway and Lorena Taylor Holloway, was then nine years old and living on the farm north of Millard.

She took a photograph of her father and mother sitting in the new Buick, a touring model, on May 7, 1916, an event she recorded in her diary. In the photograph, horses are in the barnyard and chickens are feeding on the ground. My grandfather proudly poses, one hand on the steering wheel and the other on the door. My grandmother, whom I would know only as my mother's mother, stares straight ahead. She would die seven years later of Bright's disease at the age of thirty-eight. My mother always kept a portrait of her mother on the coffee table.

The copy I have before me lacks the sharpness of the original. The negative has been lost,

W. V. B. Holloway and Lorena Taylor Holloway, May 7, 1916

and I have a print made from the snapshot that is still in the cabinet on the front porch. Nevertheless, this print will do. The past is always clouded, one way or another.

My grandfather, others called him Will, worked the family farm north of Millard. As a young man, he was elected town clerk, an office he held for fifty-six years. In midlife, he sold the farm, built the house in Millard, lost his wife, and married Mabel Johnson. He was my grandfather for twenty-five years.

When we visited him at his house, he was often seated at his desk, a green visor on his forehead and rubber bands on his arms to hold up the sleeves of his dress shirt. On summer evenings, he and Mabel would drive to the farm to visit us. In good health at the age of eighty-six, he was struck by a car and killed instantly as he walked from the corner grocery store, evening newspaper in hand.

Emigration from England is the dominant story of the ancestors on my mother's side of the family. For their history, I refer to several genealogies gathered by family members, to the obituaries found in dresser drawers and cabinets, and to the notes I have made in journals over the years.

Emigration began in the late 1830s. For the Taylors, living conditions in Penistone, Yorkshire, a few miles east of Manchester, were deteriorating. Prices were high and there was little work for the laboring class. Joshua Taylor, Jr., already in Wisconsin, wrote to his brother and sister as they were preparing to emigrate:

> I am very glad you have made up your mind to come to America. I think it will be the best move you ever made in your life. It is a foolish idea that some people get into their heads there is no place like Old England, for this is a better country than England has ever been in your days or ever will be. I have 160 acres of land. Would I have had it in England? No. If I had stayed in England and lived to be one hundred years old I would not have had one acre to call my own.

The letter continues with advice for the voyage and a listing of provisions needed for starting life in the New World.

Some years ago in the mid-1960s, I traveled to England to see the birthplace of the Holloways. James Holloway, my great-grandfather, had emigrated in 1866 to seek a life that was no longer possible on the family farm at West Buckland in North Devon. After spending the night at a bed and breakfast in Barnstaple, I took the bus to a stop near the farm and walked up the dirt road that led to the thatched, abandoned farmhouse, a place still known as Bright's Leary.

James Holloway had purchased a ticket for passage to Australia, but he changed his mind at the last minute. He sailed instead to Canada and then made his way to Walworth County. Soon he met and married Mary Bray, who had come with her family from North Petherwin in Devon. The couple moved several times, from one farm in the county to another, until James died in 1911. He is remembered in an obituary as "a devoted husband, a loving father, a kind and helpful neighbor, ever ready to do a kindly act."

On a shelf in my study is a photograph: my daughter Laura and I are standing in front of the vacant farmhouse at Bright's Leary. Above my desk hangs an auction bill for October 23, 1873, describing the possessions to be sold that day. I have heard that a family from London has since restored the house and now lives there on weekends.

Still, I am haunted by the photograph of my grandparents in the new Buick, the photograph taken by my mother in 1916 when she was nine. My mother's mother in the back seat, elegant, looking straight ahead, eyes in shadows.

3

They would marry on a day in September 1930. As you can imagine, I have always been thankful that Alice Holloway and Floyd Quinney met at a dance, fell in love, and decided to spend the rest of their lives together.

The marriage ceremony was a simple one—Floyd and Alice, their friends Mildred and Allyn Strong, and the Methodist minister. The church was located on the far side of the Holloways'

Floyd Quinney and Alice Marie Holloway, Wedding, September 15, 1930

garage in Millard. My mother was twenty-four and my father was thirty. A few photographs were taken in front of the house and in the driveway. My grandfather and Mabel must have taken the photographs. Happiness is evident in the photographs of that day in September.

They drove to Niagara Falls for their honeymoon. Each posed for a photograph in front of the falls. Years later they would tell about the trip that took them through Detroit and home again by way of Michigan Avenue in Chicago. They made certain to see the factories for Chevrolet and Ford. At one point the brakes failed on the car. Years later, my mother and father talked about driving over the tall bridge at Windsor. Recently, I found the negatives of the photos they had taken on their honeymoon in a brown envelope at the farmhouse.

Returning from the honeymoon, they moved into the house that my father had just built. The house was located next to the barn, up the hill and across the field from the old place. The house was of a California bungalow design, no doubt inspired by my father's trip to California. It would be the homeplace, the center of the world for the life that was to follow.

Their separate ways were over, melting gently away on that September day in 1930. They stand beside the gray stucco house, hands joined and smiling, looking into the noonday sun. My mother, or the woman who would become my mother in four years, had lived in the stucco house her father built. She attended high school in Elkhorn and received her teacher's training at the state normal college in Whitewater. She then began her career as a teacher in a country school, teaching all eight grades in the Bay Hill School near Williams Bay. She boarded at the Farrar farm down the road. My mother would often tell the story about walking to the schoolhouse early on winter mornings to light the wood-burning stove before the students arrived. There are photographs in her album of picnics on summer days with her friends.

My father, or the man who would become my father in four years, attended Dunham School, the grade school his father had attended and the school I would attend. He began to work the farm, helping his father, shortly after grade school. He also worked in town for a while as a weaver at the Delavan knitting mill. Years later he would teach me to tie the knitter's knot, a knot so small it could pass through the machine's needle.

I heard neighbors talk about the good times my father had known. He had owned one of the first Model T Fords in Sugar Creek Township. He had an Indian motorcycle, but gave it up after skidding and falling on the gravel road. The story of his six-month trip to California with his good friend Mervin Kittleson was alluded to many times and in many ways. In the attic of the house are the relics and souvenirs of his journey west. Returning home, he farmed for the rest of his life. He often said that someday he would like to move to town.

In the hard work of farming through the war years, I remember my father and mother as happy and content together, the kind of happiness that makes you know that they will always be together. For nearly thirty years my mother lived alone on the farm. There is a sense in the house, never mentioned, that my father and mother are still together.

4

It is my first birthday, May 16, 1935. My mother and father have carefully arranged a photograph for the occasion. I have been placed at the window of the dining room, cake and candle at my side. Either my mother or father has gone outside with the Kodak box camera to take the picture. My first birthday is recorded in natural light. The expression on my face is one of curiosity and expectation—a curiosity open to whatever may happen next, and yes, a desire to know and to accept what cannot be known.

Looking through the family album, I have no memory of the times I was posed or caught before the camera in the early years of my life. My memories are of the few times that I have seen these photographs, viewing them with my parents, with friends, with my wife and daughters. Some people easily remember themselves in events before the age of six. I only know that I had parents who cared very much for me, who savored the moment and hoped to preserve it. Photographs remain as signs of love.

The earliest event that I do remember without the aid of a photograph is my grandfather

Earl Richard Quinney, First Birthday, May 16, 1935

Quinney coming across the field and my father pointing him out to me. It must have been the summer of 1938; my grandfather would die at the beginning of the next year, when I was four years old.

Another event that I recall clearly is remembered because it was an epiphany of sorts, a calling, a vision quest. I was seven or eight years old. I was walking on the hill east of the barn. I lay down in the pasture and looked up into the sky. In the clouds appeared the face of George Washington. I was struck with awe. I knew that I had been chosen to see this wonder. A good life and good works must surely follow such a privileged experience.

The Midwest landscape that I could see—the hills and fields, the woodlands and the marsh—measured the depth and breadth of my existence. Looking to the far horizon, where the earth meets the sky, I sensed the wonder and immensity of the world.

5

With the birth of my brother Ralph on June 4, 1936, our family was complete. The Depression was on, my father and mother were farming with horses, and the farm was operating in a subsistence economy. On Friday nights, the weekly supply of eggs was traded for groceries at Kroger's. One night a leghorn hen rode to Delavan on the front bumper of the car, rested while we shopped, and rode the five miles home. We found her after we parked in the garage and began to unload the groceries. World War II was yet to come and life seemed very simple.

My father and mother photographed my brother and me in a variety of activities during our early lives. The albums are filled with snapshots of us on the lawn, in the fenced playpen, on horses, in fields, at picnics, on bicycles, with pets and farm animals, and on vacations to the northern lakes. Often my father posed with us, other times my father took a picture of us with our mother.

On Friday nights, the week's roll of film was taken to the drugstore for developing and

A Sunday Afternoon, 1937

printing and the previous week's packet of processed photos was picked up. Fortunately, my parents always saved the negatives instead of discarding them once the packet of photos was opened. I continue to print from the negatives they made in the 1930s, 40s, and 50s.

My primary interaction with another child was always with my brother, but Betty and Jimmy Gies lived on the farm down the road and Jack and Jean Harper lived on the farm to the north. We walked to school with them in the morning and played together in the evening. The rest of the time—chore time, weekends, and summer days—Ralph and I were company to each other.

During our high-school years, Ralph and I drove the truck to school in town. When I left high school for college, we went our separate ways. Although we have not spent much time together until recent years, we have always known that we can count on each other for help and that in time of need we will be together.

At the end of summer 1937, Ralph and I are seated on either side of my mother on the back bumper of the Chevy. We are dressed for an occasion, and likely we have just returned from it. The sun is getting low in the southwestern sky. Dad will soon change into his overalls and gather the cows for milking. Ma will feed the chickens and prepare supper. All seems to be in good order. My brother and I feel secure in the world.

6

It is afternoon in the middle of August 1942; I am eight years old and Ralph is six. My father was forty-two that year. A gentle wind is blowing from the west. In the field, oats are being cut and tied into bundles. My mother has walked into the field among the stubble with her camera.

The McCormick-Deering binder that once was pulled by two horses is now hitched to the Oliver 70 tractor. All day long Ralph and I cross the field, back and forth; I am driving the tractor and Ralph is on the binder adjusting the levers and releasing the bundles. I am wearing a dust mask outfitted with a battery to alleviate the hay fever that is triggered by the dusty grain.

Working in the Grain Field, 1942

I complain to my father that I am being worked too hard. I tell him that I am too young to be working, that the kids in town are playing and loafing and still being young. I sneezed all summer long in the hot and dusty field.

At the end of the month, the threshing machine will be pulled into the field and the crew of neighbors will arrive. A large tractor will be aligned to the machine for power, and the men will begin pitching bundles of oats from their wagons into the hopper of the threshing machine. Straw will be blown into a stack while chickens gather to feed on the fresh grain scattered on the ground.

The summer ends with the Walworth County Fair, where our summer of hard work is celebrated. I exhibit the Duroc hogs and the chickens that I have been raising during the summer, and Ralph shows the Hampshire sheep that he has carefully tended. A barred rock rooster that I exhibit receives the grand champion award. But the real excitement of the fair is being able to leave the farm for four days at the end of summer and to experience another world.

During the days at the fair, I walk the grounds unattended and uninhibited. Music plays in the Janesville radio station's tent. Exotic foods are abundant, and on the midway there is magic and mystery. Strange-looking carnival workers beckon. A woman in tight pants offers darts for popping balloons; a man with tattooed arms and an opened shirt holds out three balls and the challenge to down a stack of wooden bottles. Motorcycles roar as they speed around a walled enclosure. An octopus-shaped ride ablaze with colored lights reaches out into the night sky. And after waiting all summer long, I finally ask Kate Seymour to ride to the top of the Ferris wheel with me. School will begin tomorrow.

7

Dunham School was one and a half miles east of the farm. We either walked or rode our bicycles on the gravel road to school in the fall and spring. In the winter, when the snow was deep,

Dunham School, Halloween, 1946

Dad hitched the horses to the sleigh for the ride to school. Some days we rode in the pickup truck. I especially remember walking to school on spring mornings and watching water flow under sheets of ice in the ditches on either side of the road. Whatever the mode of travel, whatever the season, going to school and coming home again were playgrounds for the imagination. We thought of ourselves as travelers on a great adventure.

School was a refuge from work on the farm. Everything that took place at school was something other than work. No wonder, then, that I eventually decided to spend my life in school. Almost everything associated with education was a kind of play, a refuge from farm work. My career has been a continuation of my years in the one-room country schoolhouse.

Each grade of students had a period of class recitation in the morning and in the afternoon. We sat at our desks in the one room; we studied, and we listened to other classes reciting in a circle at the front of the room. We looked out of the large windows to the north and the west. In the back of the room, a cabinet with glass doors held the wonders of nature that we gathered on our way to school: stones, snake skins, leaves, bones, and feathers. Our museum.

We had two recesses each day. In the fall and spring we played baseball, boys and girls together, on a field in back of the schoolhouse. The paths were worn from seventy-five years of play. On other days we divided into sides and played Andy-Over the Schoolhouse, tagging each other to increase the size of our team. The old merry-go-round turned and squeaked and swung back and forth until it nearly fell to the ground. On Halloween day in 1946, the nine of us, all the students in the school, posed in our costumes. The next year, District 9 was forced to close.

8

The photograph is of a newly constructed pig house, a large structure with monitor windows to catch the afternoon sun. This one picture captures eight years of my life, from the time I

Pig House, Near Sharon, 1952

began high school in 1948 to my graduation from college in 1956. Who would believe that a pig house, I should say the making of a pig house, could mean so much?

Entering high school in Delavan was the beginning of my departure from the farm. Delavan, a town of 2,500 people, had always seemed to me to be an entry to the larger world, a world beyond the confines of life on the farm. Only five miles south of the farm by either County Trunk O or County Trunk P, Delavan had been the place we shopped for clothes and groceries, where we went to church, and where we went for hardware to repair our machinery. Fortunate was the one who rode to town during the week to make a necessary purchase.

My first year in high school was difficult, not because of the studies but because of trying to adjust to the ways of the kids in town. We who came from farms were regarded as "hicks" and "farmers," as unsophisticated and less worthy than the kids of the business and professional families in town. We were not accepted readily as friends among either the elite or the working-class kids. We struggled to be accepted by anyone outside of our own farm backgrounds. By the middle of the year, I developed severe stomach pains. I convinced Dr. Crowe that it was appendicitis and he removed a perfectly good appendix. But I immediately felt better and newly prepared to make my way in Delavan High School.

I learned to play trombone and joined the band. I became the photographer for the student newspaper. My class elected me to office. I participated in forensics and appeared in several school dramas. I learned to play golf. And I had a steady girlfriend. At the end of my senior year, the yearbook noted beside my picture, "Thou makest the sad heart gay." The high-school band marched through town to the cemetery on Memorial Day. Back in the band room, we said our goodbyes and dispersed into the day.

That was the summer that our neighbor, Burton Hanson, and I built the pig house on the farm north of Sharon. I had worked part-time during the two previous summers at the National Tea grocery store. I stocked produce, weighed and priced fruits and vegetables, and carried bags of groceries to the cars of married women. During breaks, my friend Lee Farrar and I walked to the drugstore for Cokes. The real treat was being in town on a summer's day.

Burton lived with his wife Gladys in the farmhouse on the Dutcher place, a house located on the forty acres my family had bought years earlier. While I was growing up on the farm, Burton had been the most important adult in my life other than my parents. He introduced me to the natural world beyond farming. He took my brother and me fishing along Turtle Creek after long days of haying in the sun. Once he brought me an aspen log with the marks of a beaver's teeth he'd found on a trip to northern Wisconsin. He helped my father in the fields, and he could repair any building or piece of machinery. He expressed delight and surprise with the words, "Man alive!"

Burton and I worked together building the pig house that summer. He taught me enough carpentry to be of help in completing the project. We drove from the farm each morning, ate our packed lunch at noon, and drove home at the end of the day. While working, I could see the water tower for Sharon in the distance. Now, nearly fifty years later, driving to the farm and passing through Sharon, I look for the pig house that Burton and I built, but I cannot find it. Perhaps I have yet to travel the right road, or perhaps the building has been torn down.

Gradually, over my years away at college and graduate school, I lost contact with Burton. Once I visited him at home in Maywood, a western suburb of Chicago, where he lived the rest of his life. I saw him for the last time on the day of my father's funeral. It was snowing at the graveside, and we looked across at each other. After a few moments, I saw him walk slowly to the car parked on the hill. We neither tried to speak to each other nor to renew the life that had passed.

9

I chose Carroll College in Waukesha as the college that I would attend. It appealed to me because nobody I knew was going there, but also because it was known as Wisconsin's "Pioneer College." When I had ridden to Waukesha with my father numerous times to purchase parts for the Oliver tractor, I had seen the college in the distance.

I cannot remember for certain what I learned at college. Only the generalities remain: I majored in biology and sociology; I joined a fraternity in order to live in a house; the students elected me as their president; Peggy and I broke up after my first year; and for all four years I missed my home.

When I graduated, I planned on becoming a hospital administrator. Another possibility was to become a forest ranger, but I applied to the program in hospital administration at Northwestern University and was accepted. During the summer months I had worked in Janesville at Mercy Hospital as an orderly in surgery. Carrying body parts to the pathology lab during operations convinced me that I did not want to be a medical doctor, but administering a hospital might be good, combining sociology with my knowledge of human biology.

The summer after graduating from Carroll, waiting for fall classes to begin at Northwestern, I worked for a month in the credit office of Wesley Memorial Hospital in Chicago. I failed at the task of calling former patients and threatening them with dire consequences if they did not pay their bills. Disenchanted with the helping profession, I drove up Lake Shore Drive to Northwestern's Evanston campus and inquired about graduate work in sociology. Kimball Young, the grandson of Brigham Young, welcomed me to the Sociology Department. I completed the master's degree by the end of the next summer, and I was accepted at the University of Wisconsin to work on my Ph.D. I would be able to spend my life in school.

My first Saturday night in Madison, a night in September, I walked into the ballroom at the student union where a dance was being held for graduate students. The lights were turned low, the music played softly, and a woman walked across the room in my direction. In nine months, Valerie would become my wife.

As hardworking married graduate students, we and our friends attempted to accommodate our separate worlds of work and our common lives. We took the full load of courses and worked as teaching assistants. On Friday nights, we met at Glenn and Ann's, and at other times we entertained in our apartment. Valerie soon became pregnant, and Laura Ellen was born the following spring.

Students' Observatory, University of Wisconsin, 1957

We did our best as new parents. We bought groceries and baby food on eight dollars a week. With a grocery cart and the week's laundry, we carried out the weekend chores. Early on weekday mornings, I would put two eggs on to boil, hand Valerie the baby for nursing, and after a quick breakfast hurry over the hill to the Quonset building to teach the early morning class on marriage and the family.

We left Madison on a summer morning in 1960. With our small aquamarine Renault packed, we drove to the farm for two days. Then we headed east to Canton, New York, where I would begin my first job as an instructor at St. Lawrence University. I would complete my doctorate in two more years, and Valerie would eventually complete hers. On the road east, Laura spoke her first complete sentence, "I am hungry."

After two years at St. Lawrence, I accepted a job as assistant professor at the University of Kentucky. Thousands of acres of Kentucky bluegrass fields surrounded by white wooden fences trailed beyond stately mansions. In Lexington, out of sight of middle-class houses, along the railroad tracks and behind the tobacco mills and warehouses, were the unpainted and dilapidated houses of the poor. We soon became involved in the civil rights movement, participating in local protests and demonstrations.

On a bright November afternoon, I walked downtown after teaching my sociology class. Along the way, the pace of traffic began to slow down as radios reported the first eyewitness accounts of a shooting in Dallas. Later it was confirmed that President John Kennedy had been assassinated, the shots coming from the book-depository building in Dealey Plaza. Lyndon Johnson was sworn in as the new president as Kennedy's body was flown across the country to Washington. A few days later, we watched on television the shooting of the assassination suspect, Lee Harvey Oswald, as he was being transferred from jail.

My own thinking and writing in sociology were increasingly influenced by the turmoil and changes in the country. In the basement of our rented house near the university, I constructed a study and worked late into the night beside the warm furnace. Laura played with other children in the backyards and parks near the house. I began to use my middle name after a friend told me that I was more of a Richard than an Earl. I read *The Myth of Sisyphus* by Albert Camus for the first time, and I identified with the struggle that fills the human heart.

Evening under lamplight, I look at the photographs again. There are color slides from the 1950s. We are in the kitchen of our first apartment. Turquoise plastic utensils, copper-bottomed Revere Ware, a box of Tide on the shelf, electric toaster and baker. There are photographs of Lake Mendota and the University of Wisconsin campus, photographs of visits from our parents, and photographs of Laura as a baby. I keep a box of these in my closet, and occasionally I have a print made from one slide or another.

The innocence of those days touches my heart, and the photographs bring back our early years. The following years would be mixed with the joys and sorrows of making a life together. I cannot analyze or evaluate them, nor will I judge. And I will not say what life should have been, or could have been. A divorce is, as Valerie said when we ended our marriage thirty years later, a death.

10

After three years of living in Lexington, we moved to New York City. At a meeting of sociologists, I had been introduced to the chairman of the Sociology Department at New York University. The department was looking for a sociologist to hire at the associate professor rank. Later I was contacted and asked to fly to New York for an interview. As I walk through the darkened, marble passageways of Rockefeller Center on my way to the interview in a building on Washington Square, I know that I will take the job if it is offered to me. My life has been leading up to this, to be at the center of the world. Far, far from the farm.

We leave Lexington in the middle of the summer of 1965. Laura is crying as she waves goodbye to her friends from the back window of the car. Valerie and I have not given ourselves the chance to have second thoughts about leaving. A day later, the spectacular skyline of New

East River, Manhattan, 1969

York City appears early in the morning as we drive down the Palisades Interstate Parkway. Passing over the George Washington Bridge and moving with the heavy traffic on the West Side Highway, we exit onto Twenty-third Street and make our way down to Greenwich Village.

We find an apartment on the second floor of the Washington Square Village housing complex. After three days of receiving parking tickets because of the confusing alternate-side-of-the-street parking regulations, Laura and I drive the rusting Renault over the Brooklyn Bridge and sell the car at a junkyard for ten dollars. We will not need a car in New York City.

Greenwich Village had become the home of many midwesterners in their search for literary and artistic expression. During my years in New York, I imagined their lives, visiting the places they had lived, stopping at the cafés and taverns they had frequented, and walking the streets and paths they had walked. I listened to the music on Sunday afternoons in Washington Square Park. And I began to pursue my own photography seriously, taking evening courses at NYU with Sandra Weiner. She liked my work and encouraged me. I walked the streets of Manhattan, circled the island, took the train to Coney Island, photographing daily with passion and abandon.

By the end of 1967, a half million American troops are in Vietnam. Three million tons of bombs have been dropped on the small country. Civilians have been napalmed and killed, and much of the land has been turned into a wasteland by chemical defoliation. Yet the Vietcong have not been pacified, and American casualties are mounting. The war is costing billions of dollars each year, and there are cutbacks in the Great Society programs. We are involved in the opposition to the war. In 1968, we all are stunned by the assassination of Martin Luther King, Jr.

Our work at the university is being radicalized. In my teaching and writing, I argue that our academic work is and must be political and that we can provide an understanding that promotes the necessary changes in the social and economic order. Divisions develop within the university as we are affected by the various events and debates. I am promoted to full professor, but it seems inconsequential in such times.

In other ways, life goes on in the city. We attend off-off-Broadway plays, shop for groceries at the Grand Union, walk Eighth Street and browse in the bookstores, see the latest foreign films, attend lectures and poetry readings, go to concerts at Lincoln Center, and meet friends in bars along Bleecker Street. I often go uptown during the day to museums and department stores. Laura attends P.S. 41 on Eleventh Street near Sixth Avenue, plays between the apartment buildings, and goes with her friends to Washington Square Park. On Christmas Eve, we sing under the Washington Square arch with other Villagers. On New Year's Day, we take a taxi to the Upper West Side for a festive gathering with friends.

As the 1968 presidential election nears, and Lyndon Johnson announces that he will not seek re-election, we work for Eugene McCarthy's nomination as the Democratic candidate. Robert Kennedy enters the primaries and is shot to death the night of his victory in the California primary. Hubert Humphrey becomes the Democratic presidential candidate at the party's national convention in Chicago. In the fall election, Richard Nixon defeats Humphrey by a considerable majority and becomes the next president.

But then my father dies. November 14, 1969. The following summer we live in Madison and often visit my mother on the farm. Valerie is pregnant throughout the summer, and exactly one year after my father's death, Anne is born. Back in our New York apartment, Laura welcomes the baby home with a bird-of-paradise flower. We will leave New York City the following spring.

11

My father and mother had just visited us in New York. Sitting around the dining-room table, my father announced that sometimes his heart fluttered and that he was taking medicine that the doctor had prescribed. We made light of the news; I remember telling him that he would

The Farmhouse Basement, November 1969

live for a long time. A week later, my cousin Shirley Taylor called to tell us, carefully, that my father had died of a heart attack late in the afternoon as he was making repairs on the tractor. The next day we flew to Milwaukee, where we were met at the airport by my cousins and driven to the farm. In the falling snow, my mother waited for us, standing on the lawn between the house and the barn.

One day during their visit in New York, my father and I walked to lower Manhattan. Along the Bowery we passed men sleeping in doorways of shops and abandoned buildings. That day was the first and only time I ever saw tears in my father's eyes. He had never seen such pain and desolation. Another day we all rode in a horse-drawn carriage in Central Park. The last photo of my father was taken on that ride. It is in a tray of colored slides, I am certain, on the top shelf of my mother's bedroom closet.

We took a cab in the morning to Kennedy International for their return to the farm. We rode through Chinatown and left Manhattan in the distance as we crossed the Brooklyn Bridge. At the airport, waiting on the observation deck before their departure, I was caught by surprise when my father took my hand in his, for the first time in our lives, to say goodbye.

At the funeral home in Delevan, I remained in the far corner of the room. We drove through town to the cemetery on a dark and snowy day. I remember thinking that this was the end of an era. But I was wrong—my father continues to be a presence in my life, a presence that only increases with the years. And yet the loss will never diminish.

I stayed on the farm for a few extra days after the funeral, hoping to help my mother. We shared a sense that time had stopped. I did some maintenance work on the fences, picked up around the barn, and closed the machine-shed doors. To get some relief, I did what I usually do in times of need; I photographed. I photographed what I could still find of my father: tools on the work bench, shovels in the granary, books in the attic, boots and jackets and caps in the basement, and light streaming through the windows. My mother and I spoke few words about what had happened, or about how we might yet live.

12

I cannot imagine a life without my two daughters. My adult life has been shaped by being their father. Daily life has been lived with thoughts and actions that have attended to their well-being. Photo albums and boxes are filled with pictures I have taken to capture the moments of their lives, and the very act of taking the photos has placed us in the moment of being together. On the desk before me is a photograph of Laura holding Anne, giving her a bottle. Anne is holding Laura's little finger. It is but one photograph in the evening under lamplight, and all through the day.

How can a parent speak about his or her children? What can be said? Parenthood is the one area of my life where words fail me, or rather, where everything that is important is beyond words. We know that the word *love* refers to everything that cannot be put into words. But ultimately love is a multitude of actions, a lifetime of actions, that take place without question or deliberation. One would give one's life.

I could relate stories of events in the lives of Laura and Anne, stories that play in my head daily, but to do so publicly, in writing, would be a betrayal of their own experiences. They too are writers, and they will tell their own stories. In the meantime, and always, I am grateful to be their father.

Laura and Anne Quinney, November 1970

13

We load the twenty-foot U-Haul truck with all of our belongings. I have taken a sabbatical from the university, and we have given up our apartment in Washington Square Village. Living in New York has become too much a life of consumption, cultural as well as material, and I feel out of touch with the natural world. We are already assuming that when the sabbatical is over we will not be returning to New York City.

Laura is beside me in the cab of the truck. Valerie and Anne will wait until the next morning for the flight to North Carolina. Derek Phillips, my colleague in the Sociology Department, bids me goodbye and shouts, "Have a good life!" as we pull out to the street and head for the Holland Tunnel and the highway that will take us to Chapel Hill.

Each place that I have lived has given its own character to my life. Or maybe I should say that something different and unique has taken place in my life wherever I have lived. In Chapel Hill, I had a new sense of freedom, no longer bound by the structure of employment at an institution. My life seemed to be in transition, but when is one's life not in transition? Certainly changes were taking place around me and within me. I was nearing forty, and I was free to explore a new place.

Warmer weather, the slower pace of a small town, a beautiful natural setting in the South, a good university library, an emerging circle of friends, time to think and to write, new scenes to photograph, live music in town—all these gave context and substance for a life. On weekends we had good times visiting Valerie's mother, stepfather, and father in nearby Greensboro. Laura attended the Quaker school and Anne learned to walk and talk and play with other children in the neighborhood. We lived on royalties from my books, and we bought a house on Tinkerbell Road at the edge of town.

Soon I was being invited to give lectures all around the country. I flew to speaking engagements in Montana, Kentucky, California, Minnesota, Florida, Illinois, Indiana, and New York. I became part of a community of socialists and activists. The mayor appointed me to the charter-

Chapel Hill, North Carolina, 1974

review commission. My photographs were exhibited in a gallery. I wrote and published three books. We drove to Wisconsin to see my mother on the farm, and we visited Uncle Lloyd and Aunt Elsie, who were getting to be very old.

Such is a listing of my activity, to my own amazement and bewilderment in retrospect. In the middle of all of this, our marriage was faltering. I do not know whether the problems were the cause or the result of all the activities and changes in my own life. I suspect a complex of causes beyond analysis or blame. The fact is that eventually I had to live a good part of a year in a house without my family. The sun in the morning would flow through the bedroom window and fall across the flowered wallpaper. For some reason, I recalled that Montgomery Clift drank grape juice and vodka for solace in the morning.

At the end of August 1974, back together, we moved to Providence, where Valerie had taken a job as assistant professor at the University of Rhode Island. Resigning my professorship at New York University, I would teach for the year at Brooklyn College and the Graduate School of the City University of New York, commuting between Providence and New York. The possibility of starting over was a welcome relief. We loaded the U-Haul truck, and Laura and I drove north on the interstate highway. Valerie and Anne followed in the blue Dodge Dart. We would live in Providence for the next nine years.

14

Roger Williams and a small band of Puritans had made their way from the Massachusetts colonies in the winter of 1636. Seeking a place where their community might be established, they settled near a sweet-flowing spring on a site that Williams would call Providence. He wrote, "I desired it might be for the shelter for persons distressed for conscience." On naming the settlement, Williams went on: "And having in a sense of God's merciful providence unto me in my distress called the place Providence." As a weary traveler myself, I was in search of a place where

I could renew the meaning of my life. For nine years, Providence would be that place. A well-loved place.

My explorations of mind and soul had begun. I secured a room, a study, on the top floor of the library located high on a hill at Brown University. From my window, I looked out over the city of Providence daily. Church spires mingled with the buildings of commerce and industry. To the west, Narragansett Bay opened to the Atlantic Ocean. Down the street from the library, H. P. Lovecraft had written his fantasy tales. Devoted to the place, he requested the epitaph for his gravestone at Swan Point, "I am Providence."

Writing had become an important means for me of communicating with myself, with others, and with the world. I wrote to create a reality for myself, to clarify my thoughts, and to make contact with a world that seemed inaccessible to me in other ways. I was trying to find meaning in the world and in my life.

In the writing of my book *Providence,* I made what seemed to be a breakthrough in my thinking. More than ever before, I began to combine the spiritual and the material. I was on a pilgrimage, drawn by the desire for satisfactions not supplied by the world I was then experiencing. After twenty-five years of excluding religious questions from my life, I was returning to questions that were essentially religious. The spiritual element that had been missing from both my work and my life was being renewed. Using the language of the Judeo-Christian tradition, I sensed a world filled with wonder, with what is traditionally called the divine.

We lived in a house on University Avenue. It was a comfortable and much-enjoyed house within walking distance of Thayer Street and the library. Laura attended Classical High School. My mother came to Providence for her graduation. Laura then began her years at Yale University. Anne attended nursery school and grade school. I would take her to school on the back of my bicycle and return in the afternoon for the ride home.

I taught courses at Boston College and Boston University when our finances needed to be supplemented. Valerie continued to teach adult students at the University of Rhode Island. We made friends, shopped in the stores down the street, and walked the shaded streets past eighteenth- and

Providence, Rhode Island, 1975

nineteenth-century houses. Many days I imagined myself as Leopold Bloom in *Ulysses,* wandering through the town, hearing my own interior monologue, making a world in the course of the day.

The solitary act of writing creates a certain kind of life. One cannot spend days of writing alone without having the process affect the rest of one's life. I was developing a life that required a great deal of solitude and time for reflection.

I was impressed by Montaigne's observation: We carry within ourselves the whole form of the human condition. In my journal, I record that I am attempting to bring nature into my life. I read the lines of A. E. Housman and record them in my journal: "Here, on the level sand / Between the sea and the land / What shall I build or write / Against the fall of night?" I continue to walk the hills and woodlands of Providence.

A Zen master ends the evening's dharma talk with the parting words, "I hope you only go straight, don't know, get enlightenment, and save all beings from suffering." What is this life every day but a spiritual journey into an unknown land? We seek a place where we can be at peace.

I finally make a note to myself: "I am a midwestern writer, a regional writer from Wisconsin." My life has been that of one who grew up in the Midwest, journeyed from it, and now seeks a return. On the farm, I was part of the land. In the landscape of the Midwest is a mystery that I have felt all my life. I long to return.

15

The summer of 1983 we moved back to the Midwest. During the winter, I had received a call from the chairman of the Sociology Department at Northern Illinois University. There was a job for me at the university. I had never been to DeKalb, and I took the job sight unseen. The farm was sixty miles north of town. Our financial situation was deteriorating, and I needed a full-time job. I also wanted to return to academia. I would explore anew the Midwest that I had left as a young man nearly twenty-five years before.

South Third Street, DeKalb, Illinois, 1985

A good portion of my life has now been spent in this prairie town west of Chicago and south of the Wisconsin border. How is one to know if this life could have been different if lived someplace else? We could assume, simply, that we are who we are and we become who we become irrespective of the places we live. But I know that it is otherwise, that we are intimately shaped by the places in which we live.

Returning to the Midwest, I was seeking a place that would enhance what I had known all my life as a borderland existence. A good portion of my life has been on the edge of things—one foot in both worlds, whatever the worlds might be, neither here nor there, both here and there. An existential character living in-between, everything being possible, living in a borderland that is crossed again and again, a traveler going from one town to another, from one shore to another, I am but a short drive from the farm. Going on two decades since moving back to the Midwest, I have crossed the border often.

Our worldly possessions were transported by moving van from Providence to DeKalb. We rented a house on Taylor Street the first year; bought a house on Third Street that was our home for five years, and after the divorce and a period of living in a host of rented and borrowed rooms, I bought a Cape Cod–style house at the end of Rolfe Road, across the river from the university.

Anne went away to college after she graduated from high school. Laura completed graduate school and began her teaching career. Valerie eventually moved back to North Carolina, and I married again. In such a bare sketch, the questions of happiness remain elusive and beyond contemplation.

Life here in DeKalb as I have known it is documented in my writings. Upon moving back to the Midwest, the personal essay became my form of expression. I wrote about my experiences, and writing became a way of making sense of them. The titles of the essays reflect my life in this prairie town: "Lodging for the Night," "A Traveler of Country Roads," "A Winter's Tale," "A Dark Voyage," "A House in Town," "In a Native State," "As the Days Go By," "The Loneliest Sound Is the Whistle of a Train," and "Requiem for the Living and the Dead."

You will note a sense of melancholy in all of these accounts. That melancholy is central to my life is no longer a secret nor a fact that I try to keep from myself. It goes with the territory, this borderland. I have plans to move someday.

16

On May 3, 1991, Solveig and I drove to the courthouse in Sycamore and were married by the presiding judge. We then drove the backroads to Madison and the next morning strolled through the farmer's market on the square. With a bountiful supply of fruits and vegetables, we made our way home.

We flew to Paris in June. For seven days and seven nights we walked the streets of Paris. We woke each morning to the sounds of the city. Opening the tall windows in our room at the Hotel Residence Orsay, we watched the movement of traffic and pedestrians along the rue de Lille. Morning light danced on the contours of the apartment building across the street. At the Rodin Museum we viewed the sculptures of Camile Claudel, especially a small statue of a man and a woman entwined in *La Valse,* life's brief dance.

We are good travelers, Solveig and I. We have huddled by the fireplace through a winter in New Zealand, gathered food for both sustenance and delight in the markets of Amsterdam, returned to Solveig's homeland in Norway for visits with relatives and walks in the mountains. We frequently take trips for the weekend or for the day, exploring again and again this borderland of ours.

All summer long we watch birds nesting, plant our garden, and catch a gentle breeze coming through lace curtains in the night. In the winter, the snow falls, a few birds come to the feeder, and ice gathers on branches outside the windows. A fire burns warmly and brightly. We are fortunate to be together.

Stavanger, Norway, 1996

17

My father had worked in the barn all of his life. During my life, from young to old, I have played and worked in the barn. I have watched the barn as it too has grown old. Great joy, then, the day I walked with Daniel on the hill east of the barn. Springtime, a day in May, and my grandson is taking some of his first steps here. He is beginning to explore the place that I have known for so long. I make certain that he finds the hill and the barn and that he knows something about where this life began. He makes his way, happily, across the field.

When Laura and Billy married on a September day in 1987, they took a vow for a life of truth and kindness. Since that day, I have thought often about the words that Laura recited: "For love is strong as death." I know that death is transcended when love prevails. A love is known this day on a hill that slopes gently to the marsh below. Generations have walked this land.

Daniel at the Farm, May 1997

18

The world does become stranger as we grow older. And more wondrous. And more mysterious, beyond our comprehension. This is our time under starlight, under lamplight.

I recently walked along the railroad tracks east of town. For some time I had been wanting to make a photograph of DeKalb that would give a sense of the town and my life here. In a museum at The Hague, I had seen Vermeer's painting, *View of Delft*. The perspective of the painting is from the distant shore, the river is in the foreground, the town beyond, and light and shadows from sun-lit clouds fall on rooftops. Life goes on.

The tracks lead into DeKalb. And out again. Trains speed through town night and day. Although much of my own time is spent in solitude—largely out of choice—I live in a community. It begins very close to home: Solveig and I living our daily lives together. The circle then expands outward in many directions until finally the whole world is encircled.

In town are some of Solveig's grown children and their families who now are part of my life. There are my colleagues from the university, some of whom I see regularly. There are the friends we meet in the market, at the doctor's office, in the library, and the many faces now familiar after years of living in this town.

Outside of town and in other states are relatives and friends. My mother has lived on the farm all these years; my brother and his family live in central Wisconsin; my daughters and son-in-law and grandsons are at home in other states. Solveig's other children and their families live in distant places. We have friends in other cities and countries. Much of my emotional, intellectual, and spiritual life takes place in a daily correspondence with friends and acquaintances I have known for many years.

With such a community always in mind, we are never alone. In awareness of our common affinity and fate, we all are in the world together whether or not we know each other, whether or not we will ever meet. Our communion is with all that exists, with all that has ever existed, and with all that ever will exist: human and otherwise, stones, trees, birds, and fence lines. A deeper communion into another intensity as we grow older. Truly, in our end is our beginning.

View of DeKalb, May 1997

The Gathering of Fragments

We come to know the world—no matter how limited that world may be—fragment by fragment. We do not grasp reality fully and completely. Anaïs Nin writes: "There are very few human beings who receive the truth complete and staggering, by instant illumination. Most of them acquire it fragment by fragment, on a small scale, by successive developments, cellularly, like a laborious mosaic." Only in fragments, only in the remains of fragments—and yet the fragments are everything.

In the biblical account of John 6:12, Jesus is feeding loaves of bread to a gathering of thousands on the far shore of the Sea of Galilee. When they are satisfied, he tells his disciples, "Gather up the fragments left over, so that nothing may be lost." In the spiritual realm of the mundane, nothing is lost and everything is gained. Never will we be hungry again. Fragment by fragment, our lives are lived.

January 25, Sunday

A new year, 1998, and a new life. I am now emeritus. I have been asked the question several times: "Are you keeping busy?" Easily one could be pushed into the world of the "retired," a world where keeping busy—for the sake of keeping busy—is the alternative to boredom and, ultimately, to death. How could you die if you are keeping busy? Or, in keeping busy one might avoid the great question entirely.

I am not alone in imagining other ways of living once being freed from employment. I will keep on working, living, but *busy* is not a term that I choose to use. Staying alive, yes.

February 16, Monday

A few days ago, I wrote a letter that I am sending to colleagues and friends here and abroad. It is about my current and future work:

> I will be continuing my investigations and writing on the sociology of the Midwest. I have thought for some time about a regional sociology. My inspiration for this work is the tradition of regional studies started by Howard W. Odum of the University of North Carolina.
>
> I have been inspired for a long time by the work of the photographic section of the Farm Security Administration. Under the direction of Roy Stryker, now-classic photographs were made for the period, 1935–1943. The photographers included Walker Evans, Ben Shahn, Russell Lee, Carl Mydans, Dorothea Lange, Gordon Parks, Marion Post Wolcott, and John Vachon. The photographers from the FSA provide the dominant imagery for the 1930s and early 1940s. I will be doing documentary work in studies of the Midwest.

Exploring anew the familiar place of home—this Midwest borderland.

February 17, Tuesday

Exploration is my theme—even more, my life force—these days, exploring the familiar, discovering something new in what has been there all along. I continue to carry the lines of T. S. Eliot on a tattered piece of paper in my billfold:

> We shall not cease from exploration
> And the end of all our exploring
> Will be to arrive where we started
> And know the place for the first time.

There is something ultimately existential about exploration at this stage of my life. The timing, the situation, and the condition all conspire. Eliot again, "When the last of earth left to discover / Is that which was the beginning." Home may be the strangest, and most wondrous, place of all.

February 18, Wednesday

The first documentary filmmaker, Robert J. Flaherty, lived his life as an explorer, albeit an explorer who goes far from home to learn about his human existence. *Nanook of the North* of 1922 and *Man of Aran* of 1934 are two documentaries that we continue to watch and be inspired by. In a speech delivered in the studios of the BBC two years before his death, Flaherty placed himself in the tradition of Odysseus:

> Odysseus made his journeys and then Homer wrote about them. To discover and to reveal— that is the way every artist sets about his business. All art is, I suppose, a kind of exploring. Whether or not it's true of art, that's the way I started filmmaking. I was an explorer first and a filmmaker a long way after.

In his later years, as in his youth, Flaherty explored new country. The explorer, then and now, is on the edge, discovering something new, no matter how familiar the territory.

All is borderland. And we are always on the verge of discovery. Even—and particularly— when the borderland is close to home. Home, in fact, is the first and the last borderland, where there is the most to discover, the most to lose. Our final resting place.

February 19, Thursday

I have heard it said that we live as long as we are remembered. Two months ago my friend Bruce Von Zellen died. I delivered the eulogy at his memorial service knowing that any celebration was just another way to mourn. I noted that I would rather be other places on that day: driving west with Bruce toward the Illinois border, on the run, passing the snow-covered prairie, on the way to the Trappist monastery. We would be listening to a tape of Jack Teagarden playing Duke Ellington's "Sophisticated Lady." And if not on that road, we might be listening to a CD of Stan Getz playing the tenor saxophone on "I Can't Get Started," "Stella by Starlight," and "I Thought About You." Or on a Saturday evening, our families might be together by candlelight around the dinner table.

From the beginning of my time with Bruce, I knew that I was witnessing an extraordinary life, but one cloaked in the ordinariness of the everyday. Over the years wondrous things happened.

Trained as a biologist, Bruce brought together the seemingly disparate teachings of science and the spiritual wisdom of Buddhism. He came to Buddhism the way most of us in the West come to it: out of need. How are we to bring some balance to our restless, inquisitive minds, especially ones so trained to achieve, to excel, to compete? Such minds tend to make us less understanding and compassionate than we might be.

The course thus was set in our explorations. Bruce would continue to remind us, following Krishnamurti, that the way is a pathless way. Stay close to the moment; our only reality is in the here and now. Take good care of the moment, and all will be well—and right. But then Bruce would add, "There are no *shoulds* and no *oughts*." We recited the lines of the *Dhammapada* often: "All that we are is a result of what we have thought."

Walking in Hopkins Park or sitting through the afternoon in my living room, watching birds from the window, I would raise with Bruce the latest finding or speculation from astrophysics, cosmology, cellular biology, or medical research. Bruce would often expound with great delight on a report in that morning's *New York Times.* On other days, he would say firmly, "Richard, it's

54

just thought." We read together Seung Sahn's book, *Only Don't Know.* The phrase, "only don't know," became one of our greatest understandings together. And it was always good for a laugh.

We would read and talk about the writings of Alan Watts and the poetry of the Taoists. We read aloud the Zen poetry of Ryōkan:

> My hut lies in the middle of a dense forest;
> Every year the green ivy grows longer.
> No news of the affairs of men,
> Only the occasional song of a woodcutter.
> The sun shines and I mend my robe;
> When the moon comes out I read Buddhist poems.
> I have nothing to report, my friends.
> If you want to find the meaning, stop chasing after
>   so many things.

Even with Buddhism, however, there was the fear of death. We would calm ourselves with thoughts that had become mantras to us: "No coming, no going." "No birth, no death." "All things are as they are." Wang Wei, the wandering Taoist poet of the T'ang dynasty, writes a poem at the graveside of his poet friend. He begins: "I look for my old friend. He is nowhere."

We often asked each other, "What do you know for sure?" One thing I know for sure: This old town is a lonelier town without Bruce.

February 20, Friday

So that nothing will be lost. Equally true, of course: NOTHING LASTS. But we go on living as if nothing is lost, not knowing—not even capable of knowing—the meaning of our existence: Why were we born? Why do we die? What, if anything, is beyond death?

The older I get the less I am able to find comfort in any rationalization or justification of death. Death seems to be nothing other than a disruption of precious life, an inconvenience, and greatly unfair. From this earthly perspective, any larger meaning escapes me. Or maybe this, from Gene Logsdon in his book, *The Contrary Farmer:* "Nature is a vast killing field. No bug, plant, or animal including humans can live unless other bugs, plants, or animals die. All we do is trade corporeal forms around the gaming table of existential matter." In the meantime, we do all we can to obscure the chaos and the void.

Day before yesterday I and some fellow annuitants took a chartered bus to Chicago. Our purpose was to see the Broadway musical *Beauty and the Beast.* Before the show, I had a beer and a sandwich at Hinky Dink's, the pub in Marshall Field's department store. A man next to me was saying into his cellular phone, "Hey, don't we have fun?" Pause. "Let them think what they want."

Beauty and the Beast, Disney or no Disney, is about otherness, about being different, being different together. We from the bus rooted for the beast. It is through kindness and love that we are set free.

February 21, Saturday

The winter of El Niño. Here in the Midwest temperatures are up and snowfall is down. Often there are hints of spring in the air, yet the skies are gray and the sun rarely shines. Meteorologists at the National Weather Service say that we in the Midwest are setting a record for the number of sunless days. I sit at my desk in the glow of the lamp.

With the next snowfall, followed by the sun, I will drive my car and gather fragments on film. Through the viewfinder of the camera, I will see again, awakening to the winter fields and the trees and the fence lines. Today I enjoy words from Robert Bly's poem on the kinds of pleasure:

The Gathering of Fragments

Sometimes, riding in a car, in Wisconsin
Or Illinois, you notice those dark telephone poles
One by one lift themselves out of the fence line
And slowly leap on the gray sky—
And past them the snowy fields.

There is solace at my desk this February week.

February 23, Monday

For several winters, with the coming of cold and snowy weather, I have thought of leaving the Midwest for a place with a warmer climate, a place south or west where there is no snow and no ice and no freezing temperature. But this winter, perhaps because of the mild weather, I have longed for snow. I look forward to a snow that will cover the ground, a snow that falls all night long, a snow that sparkles in the trees with the morning light.

Last week a friend wrote from his home in Santa Barbara and reminded me of my failed plans to go to California this winter. When his friends ask about me, he tells them that I find it easier to write books when there is snow outside. True, I prosper in the solitude coaxed by the snow. A cold and snowy day invites introspection and contemplation. A peace comes with a new covering of the land. This day I would welcome the snow.

February 27, Friday

In the current issue of *Doubletake,* the quarterly journal published by the Center for Documentary Studies at Duke University, I read with interest a comment made by the photographer

William Gedney. Gedney photographed American composers in the 1960s for a book that was ultimately never completed. Writing a letter to Samuel Barber, hoping eventually to photograph the composer, Gedney made this observation about his own artistic expression:

> Dear Mr. Barber,
> At the risk of disturbing you again, I will try to explain myself more fully. I am a photographer (that word "photographer" has connotations which I despise: intrusion, publicity, selling, etc.). Photography is the medium I have chosen to use to express myself, as music is yours, and I practice it no less seriously.

I feel the same way about photography as a primary form of expression in my life. And I also hope to avoid a photography that is intrusive or invasive of another's life. This ethic is one reason I photograph landscapes, and it is the reason the line from Bob Dylan's "Dignity" appeals to me: "Someone showed me a picture and I just laughed, / dignity has never been photographed."

The same issue of *Doubletake* carries an interview with Bruce Springsteen. I like his comment that although his songs may be in protest and that sometimes he is an activist, he is mainly a witness—a "concerned, even aroused observer." I think of myself as a witness to the times. My witnessing is in my writing and in my photographing. This morning I listen carefully to the Finnish Radio Symphony Orchestra's live recordings of the symphonies of Jean Sibelius to hear a composer at work.

March 6, Friday

Waiting here at home for a sunny day and for a 35mm lens to arrive in the mail. In the meantime, I make plans for my documentary project. I prepare maps and chart routes of travel, but I know that once I begin, wandering through the day will be my modus operandi.

My subject is the transition from one reality to another: the passing of an agricultural and industrial economy to another, the demise of a rural culture and the emergence of something that is beyond the suburban. Remnants of the old remain on the landscape and along the streets of small towns. Networks and patterns of the passing order mark the landscape—country roads, telephone and electric poles strung with wire, fence lines, iron bridges, the lone mailbox in front of an abandoned farm—yet the land is heavily tilled by machinery guided from satellites in the sky. New housing developments are scattered across open fields. There are mini-malls and enclosed hog-raising operations. Much is new and all is for the taking in a photograph.

Of course, to my older sensibility, the landscape is being marred and the environment is being brutalized. But the process was already underway when the first settlers converted native lands into farms and towns. The long grass was plowed under, and railroads were built over the prairie.

I will neither lament the passing of the old order nor indict the new. As a son of the middle border, I am an integral part of what has happened in the past and what is happening now. With camera and notepad in hand, I record with compassion this existence of ours. We are of the landscape, and we too change and pass on to something else. Others will record the artifacts that remain from our time on this land.

March 7, Saturday

I photograph to leave a record of what once was here. Whether the image is of fellow beings, of the material world they have constructed, or of the land they inhabited, the photograph substantiates that all this has existed. Roland Barthes writes in his book, *Camera Lucida,* that in viewing a photograph "the effect it produces on me is not to restore what has been abolished (by time, by distance) but to attest that what I see has indeed existed." The photograph is evidence.

With the photograph, we are finally left with what Barthes calls ecstasy. We stand before the image in wonder. Perhaps all photographs are about wonderment, about the ecstasy that comes in looking between the cracks, beyond the veil. We are playing in the fields of Time, and we entertain its good friend, Death. The photograph gives us evidence of time past and time passing. What once existed no longer exists except in memory or in viewing the artifact that is the photograph. In such evidence is the fact of life and death.

Barthes also prompts us to another understanding. "I am the reference of every photograph, and this is what generates my astonishment in addressing myself to the fundamental question: Why is it that I am alive here and now?" The image before us is ultimately about us. The photograph opens us to our existence, thus the importance of photography in our time. "For Death must be somewhere in society; if it is no longer (or less intensely) in religion, it must be elsewhere; perhaps in this image which produces Death while trying to preserve life." A literal death in the photograph: "*Life/Death:* the paradigm is reduced to a simple click, the one separating the initial pose from the final print." In each and every photograph, you and I (the living) face death. We die each moment to the image before us. We look at photographs, we photograph what we love and hold dear, and we entertain an end to all of this.

March 18, Wednesday

I want to write today, if only to feel that I have accomplished something. Some days are as simple and uneventful as that. Most days of late. Yet in the simplicity of the day one senses the overwhelmingness of this life. Cut to the bone, unfettered by activity, questions about life's meaning easily surface. Not only "What is the meaning of life?" but also "How do I make the most of this one life that I am given?" Am I wasting my life when I appear to be doing nothing? Aware of the insights of Taoism and Buddhism, I am assured that in doing nothing, everything will be done, and that nothing is my true reality. Still, there is the daily unease of being human.

I do know that I am an intimate part of a great movement. Without going outside of my house, I have traveled over five-hundred million miles in the last year as the earth has curved on its journey around the sun. Add to that the rotation of the earth each day and ask an astronomer about the millions of miles we travel each moment as the Milky Way moves with the expansion of the universe. No need to ask me if I have been anywhere today. Only a lack of imagination would keep me at home.

March 19, Thursday

A quotation from the first page of *A Fortunate Man,* by John Berger and Jean Mohr: "Landscapes can be deceptive. Sometimes a landscape seems to be less a setting for the life of its inhabitants than a curtain behind which their struggles, achievements and accidents take place." And on the next page, superimposed on a full-page photograph of a landscape, is written: "For those who, with the inhabitants, are behind the curtain, landmarks are no longer only geographic but also biographical and personal."

The English country doctor is the fortunate man in the book. He is fortunate in being able to serve the community. But more: "Like an artist or anybody else who believes that his work justifies his life, Sassall—by our society's miserable standards—is a fortunate man." He is a man doing what he wants. "He has an appetite for experience which keeps pace with his imagination and which has not been suppressed."

The fortunate one is able to expect the maximum from life. Such a person is of the world. Berger quotes Goethe: "Man knows himself only inasmuch as he knows the world. He knows the world only within himself, and he is aware of himself only within the world. Each new object, truly recognized, opens up a new organ within ourselves." May I be so open to the world and truly know and be myself.

My fear on this cloudy and cold end-of-winter day, now that I am released from institutional employment, is that the imagination that I have known will come to an end. I will live for a while longer, and I hope that my work will justify my life. I hope that I will have the imagination to continue to experience the world that has been given to me.

March 29, Sunday

"When was I the happiest, the happiest in my life?" James Salter asks in his memoir, *Burning the Days.* "Difficult to say. Skipping the obvious, perhaps setting off on a journey, or returning from one." Scattered other times, "among them the weightless days before a book was published and occasionally when writing it." Salter continues: "It is only in books that one finds perfection, only in books that it cannot be spoiled. Art, in a sense, is life brought to a standstill, rescued from time."

On the far side of my desk are the galley proofs of "For the Time Being," my writing of the last ten years. The book will be published this fall. For now, the weightless days of early spring, the moments of happiness at this desk, still writing, rescued from time.

March 30, Monday

James Salter is describing the death of a fellow pilot, DeShazer, who is ejected from a flaming plane and crashes to the ground when his parachute fails to open. "Arms flapping, he tumbles endlessly, his parachute, long and useless, trailing behind." Salter then writes: "Not at first, and not until you accept that you are mortal, do you begin to realize that life and death are the same thing." All the while, we are elsewhere, in the stars.

April 8, Wednesday

In the meantime, I photograph, and in the seeing sense that even in this mortal guise I am alive. As long as I have the desire to see—to compose in a viewfinder or through a lens—I am alive. I do not know what my life would be if this passion should fail. Maybe I would rest content in the aphorism of E. M. Cioran in *Tears and Saints:* "Since nothing has real substance, and life is a twirl in the void, its beginning and its end are meaningless." The photograph is finally an illusion, my attempt to stop time, to fill the void, to preserve the moment. To be alive.

April 16, Thursday

Each morning this week, for some reason I will not examine, I have listened to David Bowie singing "Rock 'n' Roll Suicide," lines about time putting a cigarette in your mouth. The clock waits patiently on our song, and we are not alone: "You're a rock 'n' roll suicide." I continue reading the galley proofs for my book.

Even when young, Albert Camus could write that "suffering is nothing, what counts is knowing how to suffer." Camus was between times, in a transitory sadness, in mental hibernation, his biographer Olivier Todd tells us. I know that suffering is the condition of our existence. The forms of suffering are all around us and within us. Each day we experience the physical pains in our bodies and the psychological anxieties in our hearts and minds. Things we do to one another become structured and establish the patterns of suffering we all know in one way or another. The end of suffering, at least the mitigation of suffering, comes only with a change in our thinking and the subsequent change in our conduct, according to the *Dhammapada.*

At the same time, the in-between time, knowing how to suffer is our business. Suffering is an art. How to do it is a creative act.

April 28, Tuesday

Tomorrow is my mother's birthday. She will be ninety-two years old. We drove up to see her last Sunday. We had tea and I planted a tree.

Time again to remember the advice that Rilke gave to the young poet: "Have patience with everything unresolved in your heart and try to love the questions themselves as if they were locked rooms or books written in a very foreign language." Then he urges, "Don't search for the answers, which could not be given to you now, because you would not be able to live them." His advice is to "live your way into the answers." These days, of late, I have been without the questions for which answers might be sought.

In another letter, Rilke states that "a work of art is good if it has arisen out of necessity." In fact, that is how art is to be judged. My need at the moment, while questions and answers remain unformed, is to take camera in hand and shape the world through the lens that both separates me from the world and connects me to it, to bring order to an otherwise unknowable universe, some peace and rest for a soul adrift. I take a few photographs on my way north to visit my mother at home on the farm.

May 4, Monday

Gregory Peck, in "self-designed semi-retirement," is interviewed in this morning's *New York Times.* His is a gracious life, we are told, at age eighty-two. When asked by the interviewer about Charles de Gaulle's famous assertion that old age is "a shipwreck," Peck replies:

> The thing I don't enjoy is self-awareness at this stage, because you start thinking about death. I'll tell you something else: In the morning, one often has such thoughts. I make a

beeline for my newspapers, and they take up two hours, and then I can roll right through the day. I try to keep things spinning. I have plans. I have correspondence. I have this one-man show to do. It's not a career anymore. But it is a challenge. Let's say, "I've got an act."

Yes, putting an act together. Getting started in the morning is the hardest part.

May 11, Monday

Saturday night we took my mother to the emergency room at Lakeland Hospital. She had fainted and fallen in the kitchen during the day. We were relieved with the diagnosis of a sinus infection. For the first time in her ninety-two years, my mother is on antibiotics.

May 18, Monday

I do not know a better way to celebrate my birthday than to spend the day helping my mother. On Saturday we cleaned the house, planted flowers, and repaired the front door. Driving to town for a dish of ice cream, my mother reminded me that I was born on the hottest day she has ever known. I came into this world at eleven o'clock in the morning. We stayed in the hospital for eleven days and were discharged with a bill for $33.00. Despite the heat, I was wrapped in a wool blanket for safe passage home.

Peter Vansittart, an English writer, confesses in his memoir, *Paths from a White Horse,* "I now see birthdays not as years, but as significant moments." I am going for the moments as well. Sixty-four is a moment, the moment I could be of help to my mother.

May 22, Friday

The flowers have been placed on the graves for Memorial Day. During the week, my mother and I visited the cemeteries—Spring Grove, Mount Pleasant, and Round Prairie—to place potted geraniums at the headstones bearing the names Holloway, Taylor, and Quinney, several generations of ancestors, the people whose lives I have heard about all of my life.

If I had the energy, and just a little more desire, I would fly to New York to see Arthur Miller's new play, *Mr. Peters' Connections.* Starring Peter Falk, the drama portrays the mind of an ailing, aging man. The reviewer in the *New York Times* writes: "When Mr. Falk squints his eyes into feline slits, his face screwed into that familiar expression that could suggest either intense concentration or mere drowsiness, it's usually the drowsiness he means to convey here." Throughout the play, the man exists in a twilight state between semi-wakefulness and eternal sleep. Mr. Peters wonders if he is awake or asleep. We all try to find a connection, a continuity in our lives, especially as we grow older. We hope for insight, and perhaps some resolution, rather than the onset of mere weariness. The squint can reflect both insight and fatigue, or simply register the ambiguity of our existence.

June 3, Wednesday

Last Friday night, I said a few words for my good friend Jack Rhoads at his retirement dinner. I presented Jack with a photograph I had taken of him a couple of weeks before, seated on his motorcycle at the edge of a road south of town, the country horizon stretching to either edge of the photograph. I quoted T. S. Eliot on the world becoming stranger as we get older, and I reminded Jack of our mutual appreciation of W. H. Auden's line about redeeming the present from insignificance. I told colleagues and guests about our days together as graduate students forty years ago.

Jack and his wife Ruth had been best man and maid of honor at my wedding in 1958. On Friday nights we had found relief and pleasure at Glenn and Ann's on West Johnson Street. Our friendship had been renewed when I returned to the Midwest in 1983. On Wednesday nights now Jack and I and Kevin Anderson and Heinz Osterle meet at the Twins Tavern. As I told everyone at the retirement gathering, Jack and I continue, happily, astride the abyss.

June 18, Thursday

I hear a quotation from Rilke this week on public radio: "Idleness fuels the imagination." A few words here and there. A photograph now and then. Doing only what has to be done. Just enough to give the right intensity and balance to the day. "Lazy, hazy days" as summer is about to begin.

I note carefully a comment made by Jack Delano in his recent autobiography, *Photographic Memories.* He quotes the photographer Paul Strand, who believes that a photographer must have "a real respect for the thing in front of the camera." That is what I attempt to achieve as well when I go out to photograph: a respect for what I see and for what I document.

Delano is motivated, as he expresses it, "by the wonder of something I see that I want to share with the rest of the world." He adds, "I think of myself as a chronicler of my time and feel impelled to probe into the depths of society in search of the essence of truth." And for me, much of truth is in existence itself. How things look is part of the truth, the world of appearance, the only world we know.

June 25, Thursday

A heat advisory this morning. Hot and humid. The flowers, especially the lilies, are in full bloom. The cardinal and the wren call and sing from the branches of the maple and the lilac.

A dragonfly lands on the basket of fresh laundry as I prepare to hang the morning wash. The clematis twines around the trellis and sends out six-petalled blossoms of purple. The yellow flower heads of the moonbeam coreopsis direct themselves to the sun. Air conditioners hum in the distance.

A simple thought for the day. I read in the *New Yorker* last night at bedtime a "Life and Letters" report on Martha Gellhorn. Born in St. Louis in 1908, she left the United States for Europe, and over a lifetime passionately reported the atrocities of war and wrote novels. During World War II, she married Ernest Hemingway. A comment is made about her life of exile: "A loner by temperament, she seems to have taken to the postwar ex-pat's life and relished never quite belonging."

Note here that I too have spent a lifetime never quite belonging. And I too have relished this form of existence. Always on the border, one border or another. Caught between the farm and the city, valuing this everyday mundane life, but always floating some distance above it. In this world but not of it. All the happiness I have known has been found on the borderland.

June 30, Tuesday

Last Saturday night we listened to "Jazz in the Night." A short walk from the house, lawn chairs in hand, we crossed the bridge and walked to the lagoon. It was a hot summer night. Others sat in circles as candles glowed in the darkness. Steve Turre on trombone, Ron Matthews at the piano, Peter Washington on bass, and Lewis Nash at the drums. Free-floating compositions of Yusef Lateef, a few jazz standards, and some original charts by Turre. Geese, wild and domestic, floated in a phalanx on the lagoon. A summer evening in the park.

As I remember it, in the movie of the Paul Bowles novel, *The Sheltering Sky,* the narrator hauntingly observes, "Because we do not know when we will die, we get to think of life as an inexhaustible well, and yet everything happens only a certain number of times." Then he asks,

"How many more times will you watch the full moon rise?" He answers his own question, "Perhaps, twenty. And yet it all seems limitless." Such nights in the park seem inexhaustible; we could sit together and listen to music forever. And yet, I know—as the thought keeps coming into my mind—that everything happens only a certain number of times in one's life and sometime the light will go out and the night will pass. On this night, with chairs in hand, we cross the river one more time and walk home.

July 5, Sunday

An obituary appears this week of a leading exponent of the "death of God" school of theology. Paul Matthews van Buren asked how one could speak meaningfully about a God for whom no sensory verification is possible. With God-talk ruled out, he focused on the ethical behavior of the historical Jesus of Nazareth.

What we have in our time is the reality of everyday life. Our faith is in the significance of this life as a thing in itself. We may be a part of something greater—the evolution of the universe or the evolution of universes from other universes—yet, when faced with the prospect of individual death, the notion of our place in an inanimate, mathematical universe is not comforting. You and I have become attached to this conscious, embodied life of ours. I cannot imagine anything else. The thought of death strikes terror in us, but we live with the terror rather than believe in a personified being called God. Such is the ethos of our time, and the courage to live or to die.

July 7, Tuesday

A retrospective exhibit of the paintings of Pierre Bonnard has opened at the Museum of Modern Art. Bonnard lived the last part of his life in a house overlooking Cannes. He died in 1947 at the age of seventy-nine. Repeatedly over the years, he painted intimate scenes of his own domestic life. He drove through the countryside in his car, stopping to sketch, and he lived in relative isolation from other artists, preferring the seclusion of his home and studio.

In the catalog of the current exhibit, Sarah Whitfield ends her essay with the following observation: "He has often been described as a painter of pleasure, but he is not a painter of pleasure. He is a painter of the effervescence of pleasure and the disappearance of pleasure. His celebration of life is one side of a coin, the other side of which is always present—a lament for transience." Bonnard's primary mood was that of elegy. Eventually, I want to think more about Bonnard, study his life and his work, and photograph my life with his in mind.

July 8, Wednesday

So that nothing may be lost. But what, and how much of anything, can ever be remembered? What we remember at any given time is a new reality. Hamlin Garland, the self-proclaimed "son of the middle border," recalled his early years in the Midwest in a book that he titled *Back-Trailers from the Middle Border*. On the play of memory and the past, Garland wrote, "Some say it is all an illusion, this world of memory, or imagination, but to me the remembered past is more and more the reality." In this sense, it is not a matter of losing the past, but the gaining of a new reality in the present.

In his earlier book, *A Son of the Middle Border*, published in 1917, Garland wrote about his remembered childhood in the Midwest. The magic of the former time was lost forever. It could not be otherwise:

> It all lies in the unchanging realm of the past—this land of my childhood. Its charm, its strange dominion cannot return save in the poet's reminiscent dream. No money, no railway train can take us back to it. It did not in truth exist—it was a magical world, born of the

vibrant union of youth and firelight, of music and the voice of moaning winds—a union which can never come again to you or me, father, uncle, brother, till the coulee meadows bloom again unscarred of spade or plow.

Memory is the poet's reminiscent dream. A new reality.

Two summers ago, we drove north to Hamlin Garland's boyhood home in West Salem, Wisconsin. We drove into the coulee country where his parents and grandparents had lived. Later in his life, Garland purchased a house in West Salem for his aging parents. Still later, he lived with his family in the house during the summer. He called the place "Homestead."

I visited Garland's study and library on the second floor of the house in West Salem. I stood behind his homemade writing desk, and I carefully handled the small brass statue of a buffalo he had kept on the top of the desk. I looked through the window, through the glass he must have looked through as he wrote his memoirs. In the cemetery on the hill, a cast-iron sign on a post reads: "A Son of the Middle Border is buried here with his wife and pioneer parents."

I have opened *A Son of the Middle Border* to a page at random. Garland is commenting on the places of his youth. He is recognizing the "hard and bitter realities" of life in those places. A question posed by Garland jumps from the page: "What is it all about, anyhow, this life of ours?" To exist and to write about it, certainly, at least.

July 9, Thursday

Not to be forgotten. This week Roy Rogers died at his ranch, the Double-R-Bar, in Apple Valley, California, at the age of eighty-six. Whenever a new movie starring Roy Rogers was released, my father would take me and my brother to it on Friday night at the theater in Elkhorn. The author of the obituary in the *New York Times* describes the meaning of Roy Rogers to us in those midcentury years:

He was an outsized and, for a cow-poke, an immaculately dressed figure. There were his double-creased white cowboy hat, the flowing kerchief knotted at the side of his neck, the gabardine cowboy shirt, the western-cut trousers and those shiny, pointed cowboy boots. He embodied unmistakably wholesome values and evoked a vanishing and idealized America, when men tipped their hats to the ladies and sang sentimental ballads around the bone-warming glow of a campfire.

To this day, I keep a framed photograph of Roy Rogers on the wall of my study. He is sitting on a rail fence, Trigger at his side, the aura of a former time, still timeless in my life.

July 10, Friday

Yes, it is true I have courted solitude in my life, as do scholars and artists. Continuing to live in DeKalb, when I could live anyplace in the world, is a continuation of this mode of living. I remain in many ways freshly alone, unsettled. I am in great sympathy with the Nietzsche that Lesley Chamberlain describes in *Nietzsche in Turin*. Viewing the world as essentially illusionary, Nietzsche tried to find ways of seeing that state of affairs positively. "He did it by viewing life as a form of art, built upon willful deceptions and incorporating transient meanings." We humans are creatures who create our own worlds. Truth is a matter of appearance. But then we all, as Chamberlain notes, "more or less configure our circumstances so as to make them satisfying."

Turin was the right place at the right time for Nietzsche. It was the spring of 1888, his last year as a sane man. Chamberlain writes, "The place already contained his thoughts and as I have suggested it came to him like another person, a person he had long sought because he or she would be, must be, close to him." Here his real work would be done. He would recreate himself as an artist creates a work of art.

If Nietzsche represents the alienated artist, then I too am such a person, cultivating solitude and living in a place apart from other writers, from other artists. But I still ask, daily, with my usual sense of transience, Might I be elsewhere? A place where my solitude might be broken more often to the advantage of a more intense and creative life? Where I might be with others during the day, where I might venture out for beauty and for inspiration, where I might help others in some tangible way? And where might that place be? Often I know it is right here where I am now.

July 15, Wednesday

Summer is truly here on the border of northern Illinois and southern Wisconsin. The hot and humid days of mid-July, the harvesting of winter wheat, the round bales of straw in the fields, the corn about to tassel—all these are the familiar signs of a Midwest summer. Yesterday I bought a dozen ears of sweet corn at a farmstand on Highway 38.

Laura and Billy and my little grandson Daniel flew from Boston for a visit last weekend. Two and a half years old, Daniel moves rapidly about and talks continuously in complete sentences. On Saturday, we drove to the farm and picnicked on the lawn beside the house. I photographed Daniel with his great-grandmother, and on a walk down the road, I photographed Laura and Daniel with the barn in the distance.

Daniel and I explored the interior of the barn: whitewashed walls now peeling, dusty cow stalls, rusting stanchions, and gutters filled with musty straw covered in the droppings of skunks and raccoons. Daniel slept for thirteen hours following our return from a day at the farm. I have become used to being called "Grandpa."

July 30, Thursday

We drove up the lane in the tall grass, lilac bushes on the left and rows of corn on the right. My mother and I were heading for the old barn on the farm that once had been her home.

My grandfather had bought the land to increase his acreage, and the barn and an abandoned house went with the purchase. He had stored machinery in the barn when he farmed there at the beginning of the century. My mother asked me to photograph the barn. Such was our task on a summer afternoon.

It was not an afternoon to be worried by Nietzsche's central quest: How to make life bearable once we grasp what it is really like. Rather this was a day for the enhancement of life by what Robert Thurman calls the soul of enlightenment:

> It is a conscious act of making one's own life purposeful and, by experiencing unconditional love and compassion, of easing the suffering of others everywhere. From the moment one attains this grand conception, one has an inexhaustible well of hope and optimism. One must become open to the prospect of boundless future existences.

This separate and suffering self finds contentment in the awareness of an interdependent and inseparable existence. The self becomes a part of everything else. And when we realize that all is impermanent and without substance, we relax into the day and find pleasure in each passing moment.

My mother watched from the car as I carried the equipment up the hill and photographed the old barn from many angles, not so much to preserve, which would only enhance the suffering of loss, but to be together on a summer's day.

August 3, Monday

A weekend of repose, lying on the sofa reading. Drifting through the day without note of time or responsibility, no difference of opinion on what we could or should be doing. We agree that this weekend is worthy of being bottled and placed in the cellar for aging.

The substance of my reading this weekend is an antidote to a life I have fashioned. We restless and inquisitive ones, at least some of us, have turned to Eastern philosophy and meditation to calm a dominant part of ourselves, to rein in the ego, to slow the pace of our lives, to be more compassionate in our everyday relationships. In the literature of my profession, I am called "a practicing Buddhist." Of late, my practice has been modest, but what I have learned from years of practice is an integral part of my being. When the student is ready—restless and vaguely aware—the teacher appears.

I have been engrossed in reading Geoff Dyer's book, *Out of Sheer Rage,* not an academic exercise in literary criticism but an account of his own life in the course of thinking about writing a book about the life of D. H. Lawrence. Dyer prefers "the epistolary monologue" of the letters Lawrence wrote during his life to the novels that attempt to make fiction out of life. "The fact that Lawrence wrote *Lady Chatterley's Lover* means next to nothing to me; what matters is that he paid his way, settled his debts, made nice jam and marmalade, and put up shelves."

In Lawrence's letters—and in Dyer's book—the central focus is, as Lawrence expressed it, "How can we most deeply live?" "And the answer is different in every case," Lawrence added. Dyer, like Lawrence, is often discontented, enraged, and despairing. Dyer quotes Camus on the matter: "There is no love of life without despair of life." Writing is a way of dealing with despair and a way of going beyond it. Contentment comes in the writing, in the living that is accounted for in the writing.

Keep writing. Could I do otherwise? Solveig told me long ago that life is in the living of it. And in the writing, the living is fully known. Attention is given to the moment. Living and mindfulness are one.

It is noon now. A beer taken to the backyard tastes very good. Starlings are eating berries in the hackberry. On the patio: a wrought-iron table, four chairs, and pots of geraniums and marigolds. I talk grandly about the meaning of life, but what it amounts to is "one little individual," as Lawrence wrote in Mexico, "looking at a bit of sky and trees, then looking down at the page of his exercise book." This is what one also means about life in DeKalb, Illinois, on a day in August.

August 12, Wednesday

The doldrums of August. It is like being near the equator—abounding in calms, occasional squalls, and light shifting winds; a spell of listlessness or despondency. The dictionary definitions nicely describe the doldrums of mid-August this year.

I believe that I could sleep soundly at night if not for the constant humming—now a roar, it seems—of neighbors' air conditioners coming into my open window. Even the sounds of the crickets and the frogs and the cicadas are stressing my inner ear. Some nights I take to the basement for some relief. Solveig says she understands.

The corn in the field has crested this week, and thus so has summer. Most of the pollen has fallen to the silky ears, and the tassels are now nearly bare. The sweet corn has matured earlier than usual this summer due to the warming effects of El Niño. However, I am off the sweet corn this year, in part to reduce the carbohydrates in my diet. My mother reminded me again that her doctor says that corn is for pigs, but maybe cutting out sweet corn this year is also a protest. I am feeling a bit stuck on the border.

August 21, Friday

Accompanying a photograph of Carlos Fuentes, taken by Sally Soames and reproduced in her book, *Writers,* is a quotation by Fuentes: "One lifetime is not sufficient. Many existences are needed to fulfill one personality." He adds, "Reality is a sick dream."

Watching an old black-and-white movie in the basement the other morning, I heard Charles

Boyer ask Ingrid Bergman, "Does the wind know it rained last night?" What is past is past. They are standing by a window in a room in Paris.

Earlier this week I was presented with a plaque for my years of service to the university. My friend Bill Minor, chair of the department, graciously prepared the words engraved on it: "Gentle Soul. Pathbreaking Scholar. Inspirational Teacher—YOU LIVED WHAT YOU TAUGHT."

Fragment by fragment, we live our allotted days.

September 2, Wednesday

Yes, September. A leaf turning color here and there. Cooler nights. A Zen-like feeling of emptiness. Zen mind, beginner's mind. Room in the cup. These few precious days remind me of you.

A condition of the mind. Being melancholic is different from being depressed, James Atlas tells us in a recent essay on Saul Bellow in the *New Yorker*. Bellow's character Herzog offers the thesis that "people of powerful imagination, given to dreaming deeply and to raising up marvelous and self-sufficient fictions, turn to suffering sometimes to cut into their bliss, as people pinch themselves to feel awake." For Herzog, as well as for Bellow, suffering is redemptive, "a more extended form of life, a striving for true wakefulness and an antidote to illusion." I too am constantly redeemed by melancholy.

W. G. Sebald, in his new book, *The Rings of Saturn,* likens the mental condition of the weavers of silk to the mental state of scholars and writers:

> That weavers in particular, together with scholars and writers with whom they had much in common, tended to suffer from melancholy and all the evils associated with it, is understandable given the nature of their work, which forced them to sit bent over, day after day, straining to keep their eye on the complex patterns they created.

The fact is that writing—the kind of writing I am engaged in daily—is a way of coping with all the stuff of one's life. With memories, especially. Sebald writes, "What would we be without memory? We would not be capable of ordering even the simplest thoughts, the most sensitive heart would lose the ability to show affection, our existence would be a mere never-ending chain of meaningless moments, and there would not be the faintest trace of a past." And I would add, we also write to redeem ourselves in the present moment, to assure ourselves that we do in fact exist, that our existence has meaning. I write, therefore I am.

September 4, Friday

Night before last at suppertime, UPS delivered to the door thirty copies of my new book, *For the Time Being*. I opened the box and saw the book for the first time. Ten years in the making. On the cover is my photograph of the willow branches over the water of the lagoon near our house. W. H. Auden's lines on redeeming the Time Being from insignificance serve as the epigraph.

> In the meantime
> There are bills to be paid, machines to keep in repair,
> Irregular verbs to learn, the Time Being to redeem
> From insignificance.

The book is dedicated to my father, in remembrance.

Yesterday I traveled to the Walworth County Fair in Elkhorn, Wisconsin. The fair had been my yearly vacation from the chores of farming when I was growing up. My mission this time was to photograph the fair, hoping for an image or two that I might take home. The fair and the carnival within the fair speak to something mythological in our being. Nietzsche knew this well. A play with reality, a release from convention, life on another plane. I photographed the Ferris wheel, sideshows and amusement stands, chickens and horses, and fellow fairgoers in search of a good time.

On this day for senior citizens, my cousin Gail and her husband Dale were selling used books in the park for the county historical society. Dean and Shirley and Joyce, my Taylor cousins, were working at the food tent for the LaGrange Methodist Church. I told a young woman in the barn for small animals that fifty years ago I had won the grand champion ribbon for a rooster I had raised and cared for all summer long. This year, as I walked the midway before heading home, I thought seriously about having a blue tattoo engraved on my arm. I settled instead for the impermanent readmission stamp I was branded with as I walked through the gate.

September 22, Tuesday

I have been thinking, preparing for the next stage. Enough of the past with its lamentations. On with life. But how will I move on? Answer: by what sustains me always, call it art—an affirmation, a giver of life, and connective tissue to the larger world, a world beyond self yet through the self.

The reviews of a retrospective of Mark Rothko's paintings allude to the direction one should take. It is in the pursuit of one's art that the depth and sincerity of life is made manifest. Rothko is appreciated today for the estheticism of his work, for his cultivation of beauty. In the search for beauty, he was able to transcend, escape from, personality.

I think also of Harry Callahan, now in his eighties, walking the streets and parks of Atlanta, photographing wispy clouds drifting over the city. I recall his earlier photographs of waves breaking ceaselessly on the shores of Cape Cod, daily observations elevated, transformed, and transfixed by living in the depths of an esthetic vision. Truth, beauty, and a moral life.

The clouds are right, the sun is bright in the cool September air, and I have my sights on a landscape only a few miles out of town, a landscape Cézanne would have painted. I will gather my equipment and take to the road. The earth moves in a vast universe.

September 30, Wednesday

No longer the long, discursive analysis, I now confine myself to the short form, the aphorism— a concise statement, a truth briefly noted. Although the long form has its place, as in a symphony, for example, it is the shorter form that speaks to me and for me. In music, I listen intently to the preludes, the interludes, the nocturnes, the brief adagios.

I refuse to think systematically. I am open, instead, to experimental thought, to thought as it occurs, fleetingly. Short compositions within a general theme, the way a few philosophers write. Thus my attention of late to the writings of Pascal, Nietzsche, and Cioran.

Small-scale compositions that make up the larger work is the form that Milan Kundera advocates in his book *Testaments Betrayed,* whether in music, philosophy, or the modern novel. Kundera quotes Nietzsche: "We should neither conceal nor corrupt the actual way our thoughts come to us. The most profound and inexhaustible books will surely always have something of the aphoristic, abrupt quality of Pascal's *Pensées.*"

Brief thoughts come to me in the course of my daily life. Experiences—in mind and body— take form in the writing of a few words. Words that help make a life.

October 6, Tuesday

I have returned from a four-day trip to New York City. My primary objective was to study the paintings of Pierre Bonnard on exhibit at the Museum of Modern Art. Now I can be confident in my thoughts about Bonnard and his life of painting as I photograph the Midwest landscape.

I am inspired by Bonnard. His daily life was the subject of his art. He lived simply and privately. He gave free rein to the subjectivity of vision and to the ambiguities of visual experience. He reserved the margins of his paintings for the most important—and fragmentary—imagery. Still life and landscape appear together on the same canvas. Interiors, self-portraits, and Marthe in her bath. His art carried him to the very last days of his life. Life and art were inseparable.

Turning to Bonnard and traveling to New York, I am once again relieved of this compelling Midwest mentality that the world is happening somewhere else. I am reminded that the world is here as well, and especially so in this borderland. This borderland between northern Illinois and southern Wisconsin is a land that is part of the whole world.

November 6, Friday

Boarding an airplane for Paris, one is without expectation. The thinker is without thought. A time to travel. An opening to the world. The pleasure of visiting one's daughter. The good wishes of friends and family at home.

Even as I traveled high in the sky across the Atlantic, other lands beckoned. A call had come recently from a friend asking me to accompany him to India and Nepal. To Kathmandu, the most exotic place one can imagine.

Elsewhere. Places beyond the Midwest. Still, it is the borderland that continues to be the most unknown of places, where all is possible, where I live daily.

December 18, Friday

I have gathered myself daily in this study of mine. This room on the first floor, built as an annex by another householder for other purposes years ago, is an extension of myself and makes this life possible. I am reminded of the importance of the study in my life as I read Dora Thornton's *The Scholar in His Study.* The book documents the emergence of the study as a special room in homes of the Italian Renaissance. It was both a place and an ideal: "Reading, studying and thinking were considered by Renaissance writers to be free and pleasurable pursuits which gave shape and elegance to one's leisure, so that a study represented the ideal of making the pleasures of thinking and working continuous with the rest of one's existence." The place where the language of the inner life may be heard, a sanctuary for the inner life, an inner life that is one's spiritual life as well. Now there is less of the heavy weight I felt only a short time ago. My mood of late has lightened, lightened blessedly as it did once for William Wordsworth a few miles above Tintern Abbey:

> that blessed mood,
> In which the burthen of the mystery,
> In which the heavy and the weary weight
> Of all this unintelligible world,
> Is lighten'd.

Perhaps simply as I grow older will come awareness and some wisdom. This unintelligible world is appreciated and enjoyed as it is. A blessed mood at year's end.

Backyard, Rolfe Road

Elva, DeKalb County

Poplar Grove, Boone County

The Farm in May

Muskrat Pond on the Farm

Wiring to the Chicken House

Old Barn on the Holloway Farm, North of Millard

Cherry Valley Road

Highway X, West of Allens Grove

Central Park, New York

Île de la Cité, Paris

Kitchen Window, Rue du Plâtre

Residence of Albert Camus, Rue Madame

Machine Shed on the Farm

Annie Glidden Road, North of DeKalb

At the End of Rolfe Road

A Borderland Almanac

The last year of the 1900s and the sixty-fifth year of my life. We mark our time arbitrarily, by a calendar. Days into months, months into years, and years into centuries. Someplace in the scheme of days and months and years and centuries we find ourselves existing.

Where were you before you were born? a Zen master might ask. And where will you be when you no longer exist in this form? A brief moment of mortal existence, to be certain, and more a wonder for all of that. Struck by awe and incapable of fully knowing the meaning of our existence, we go on. Our faith is in the wonder.

In the meantime, on the borderland of existence, we keep records and make our notes, an almanac for the year.

January

January begins with a blizzard that fills the roads and highways with snow and closes the runways at O'Hare International Airport. Keeping ahead of the storm, Solveig drives me to the airport for the afternoon flight to London. With goodbyes to last for the month, Solveig leaves the terminal for the two hour ride home as the storm advances from the west. By evening the storm will bring a foot of snow and temperatures will fall well below zero.

The wings of our airplane—a Boeing 777—are carefully de-iced. Soon we are rolling down the runway marked by small blue lights in the snow; the engines roar, and we take to the air.

The lights of Chicago flicker below, and we fly into the dark sky over the black waters of Lake Michigan. Airborne, I am on my way to other lands.

On the ride to O'Hare, we make joint resolutions for the new year, something about mindfulness and appreciation of life. I muse over my reasons for travel, pondering the purpose of this trip to India and Nepal. I say that travel is part of my daily work, rather than merely a diversion from my life. I admit that I welcome new thoughts and insights, that I am ready to have my sensibilities shaken up a bit, to be stimulated by something new. I move outward to travel inward. Spiritual renewal—the sense of being alive, the heightening of wonder—is always a blessing whenever and however it may come.

I have been to the Hindu lands before—in mind and spirit. The Vedic texts—the Upanishads and the *Bhagavad Gita*—have shaped my thought and daily life for the last twenty years. I am not now on a spiritual quest or pilgrimage to the Hindu temples. More likely this travel is to see the physical sites where the ancient wisdom is still practiced.

Over the Atlantic I read about the travels of others to India. Carl Jung is quoted in the book that I am reading on this flight, Jeffery Paine's *Father India:* "I think, if you can afford it, a trip to India is on the whole most edifying and from a psychological point of view, most advisable, although it may give you considerable headaches." Possibly this is a warning of things to come.

A day later I am sitting in the coffee shop of the Centaur Hotel near Delhi International Airport. It is four in the morning and I have had little sleep since leaving home. Already I am into the dust and haze of India, and the allergy that I had almost forgotten about has returned. There is a smell of mold in the room. A roach darts across the night table. I am still confused from the chaos at the airport, yet because I expect very little, I might see and know the world as I am living it. And I will not be disappointed if, this time, there is nothing to be found.

Confusion, disorientation, and reorientation would be enough for this traveler. Jeffery Paine makes an observation about Christopher Isherwood's life in Hollywood. Isherwood was also a traveler to India. "Doubt was his meat and uncertainty was his drink, and he was in a strange land." My life is an experiment, guided by practice rather than certainty. Perhaps I have come this far to revive my doubts and my ambiguities. A holy mind is an open mind, a Buddhist master once told me. A small black-and-yellow ant-like insect climbs up the edge of my napkin on the early morning table.

In a small airplane operated by Royal Nepal Airlines, we fly from Kathmandu to Pokhara. The great snow-capped Annapurna of the Himalayas rises to our right as we fly west over the valleys and the foothills. Below are villages and terraced fields. My mentor and collaborator for the last forty years has convinced me that I should accompany him to the places in Nepal and India that have been important to him all of his adult life. Much is being lost on me already, as I suffer from jet lag, loss of sleep, and a persistent allergy. My bodily experience is dominating this trip, and I am feeling vulnerable and homesick. Another night I will stay awake and pace the floor of the hotel.

In the morning sky, black kites spread wide their wings and soar above the town. White clouds drift across the sharp peak of Machhapuchhare, the sacred mountain of Nepal. Facing the mountain, we take our breakfast in the dining room of the New Hotel Crystal. In the afternoon, we walk and photograph the dusty streets and alleys of Pokhara. I note that evening in my journal that there are some places in the world that we need not visit, not because of the places or the people but because of who we are and why we, removed from the life of such places, visit them as tourists. The unreality of this trip is becoming obvious to me.

If our lives were not so comfortable we would not travel to Pokhara. As for me, I do not have a romantic need for the exotic, for the otherness of the Third World. I have no desire to encounter, as Pico Iyer notes, the refuse of my own civilization dumped elsewhere. And I fear that I might become ill so far away from home.

Before dinner, where we will be watched over by attentive waiters like guards, we take a walk along the street that runs west of the airport. This must be the street that Peter Matthiessen walked and described in his book, *The Snow Leopard,* before making his climb into the Himalayas:

These edges of Pokhara might be tropical outskirts anywhere—vacant children, listless adults, bent dogs and thin chickens in a litter of sagging shacks and rubble, mud, weeds, stagnant ditches, bad sweet smells, vivid bright broken plastic bits, and dirty fruit peelings awaiting the carrion pig; for want of better fare, both pigs and dogs consume the human excrement that lies everywhere along the paths.

I have decided that I will end my trip as soon as possible, I will make my escape when I return to Kathmandu. India and Nepal will always provide spiritual grounding for my life, but given my allergy, the physical conditions, and the problems of traveling as a tourist, I will worship from afar. I know enough of the world to realize that suffering of one kind or another exists everywhere, and I do not need to view the suffering of others as a tourist. My traveling companion will continue on, on his own pilgrimage. Properly reoriented and enlightened, I will return to my own borderland.

About to make a hasty retreat from Kathmandu, I am told that next time I should read the travel guides more carefully. On the airplane from Pokhara to Kathmandu, before riding to the center of the city in a taxi along the narrow streets with handkerchief pressed to my face, I have read the description in the Lonely Planet guidebook:

> For many people, arriving in Kathmandu is as shocking as stepping out of a time machine—the sights, sounds and smells can lead to sensory overload. There are narrow streets and lanes with carved wooden balconies above tiny hole-in-the-wall shops, town squares packed with extraordinary temples and monuments, markets bright with fruit and vegetables and a constant throng of humanity. Then there's the choking dust and fumes, stinking gutters, concrete monstrosities, touts, Coca-Cola billboards and maimed beggars.

From the Yak and Yeti Hotel, I take the ride back to the airport. With the ingenuity and the skill that I had forgotten I possessed, I find a flight to Delhi on Indian Airlines. After a night in Delhi, I wait as a standby for the afternoon flight to London.

104

I fly on Air Canada for ten hours at forty thousand feet above the deserts and mountains of many countries. Near the end of the flight to London, I am transported by the music video being played on the monitor above me, Natalie Merchant singing "Break Your Heart": "I know that it will break your heart / The way things are / And the way they have been / . . . / It's enough to make you lose your mind." Arriving in the evening at Heathrow, I am ready for a good night's sleep at the Forte Crest.

The next morning I take the Underground to the center of London. I have a full English breakfast at Charing Cross and spend the morning at the National Gallery where I stand for a long time before Caravaggio's *The Supper at Emmaus.* At noon I go to St. Martin-in-the-Fields to hear a Russian pianist play Rameau, Bach, and Beethoven. At the National Portrait Gallery later in the afternoon, I see Richard Avedon's photograph of W. H. Auden. Back at the Forte Crest in the evening, I watch the BBC.

The next morning I am on a United Airlines flight to Chicago. With nothing to declare, I pass through Customs and find Solveig, waiting to take us home.

The end of January, and we have had several nights of thawing snow and gentle rain. This is the time, as Aldo Leopold described it fifty years ago in *A Sand County Almanac,* "when the tinkle of dripping water is heard in the land." Animals stir from their sleep; I see an opossum scurry under the wooden fence in the backyard. By day, three squirrels climb along the limbs of the maple tree. Chickadees, sparrows, and juncos forage among the wet seeds thrown earlier across the patio. A brown creeper probes the bark of the maple tree. Yesterday, a pair of robins rested in the hawthorn bush, and this morning, starlings are chirping somewhere in the chimney. The curiosity of this observer stirs with the January thaw.

Buddha Shrine at the New Hotel Crystal, Pokhara, Nepal

Streets of Pokhara

Bird Nest in Winter, Rolfe Road

February

The month of February, this year without a full moon. Last month there were two full moons, and next month there will be another two. But in this month of February, we will have no full moon at all. A month of earthly matters.

The newspapers report that the planet Earth is the warmest it has been in 1,200 years. The opening days of February oscillate between temperatures in the fifties and temperatures in the teens. Wind chills fall below zero, and the warming sun melts the snow on the high ground. There is talk that the sister of El Niño, La Niña, is causing far-flung changes in the atmosphere. We are experiencing the effects of an abnormally cold pool of water that stretches across the equatorial Pacific. La Niña is not so familiar to us as her brother, and her impact is less predictable, government scientists report, thus the unusual run of weather this February. La Niña is being stirred by the warming of the globe. And the jet stream—that high river of air that flows west to east—rises and falls across the borderland. There is promise of winter storms yet to come.

I wait, much like a farmer waits for the rains to come so that the crops will grow. There are photographs that I want to make when the land is covered with snow. Each day I listen to the weather reports with hopes of snow. At home, as a farmer might read seed-company brochures, I read the catalog that accompanies the exhibit of paintings I saw in the Phillips Collection in Washington last fall, *Impressionists in Winter: Effets de Neige.* I study the winter paintings of the French impressionists, Monet, Renoir, Pissarro, Sisley, Caillebotte, and Gauguin, and I think about their lives, why and how they painted, what they saw and imagined in the winter light. This year I welcome the winter. As would an impressionist.

———◆———

Rain, rain this February day is for a crop other than mine. Yet a day is what you choose to make it. I will walk uptown to post some letters.

This town in which I live is defined in the census as a city. We are a population of about 38,000. The town was created to serve an agricultural community in the nineteenth century. With the invention of barbed wire and the growth of several industries, immigrants from various nations came here to work and to live. A state college was founded that grew into a university with 20,000 students.

Still, when I walk to the center of town, I have the sense that I am living in a village: white wood-framed houses; churches of major and minor denominations; cemeteries on each side of town; the library, the city hall, the post office. A highway that stretches from coast to coast serves as the main street and an interstate highway passes just south of town. Freight trains of the Union Pacific rumble and roar through town, horns blasting, all day and night. New subdivisions with names like the Bridges of Rivermist are being built on the outskirts of town.

I sense the smallness of this place because so little of the downtown remains. Stores are empty and large buildings have been abandoned. A new urban form is being created in the developing sprawl west of Chicago. The ending of a century, the ending of an age. This is our own *fin de siècle,* a certain malaise, anxiety, uncertainty. With other villagers, I am part of the coming of a new century.

We wait. We wait and we dream. We wait for what is about to happen. We moderns—and postmoderns—anticipate another time. We wait, ultimately perhaps, for what Auden called the eternal guest, some direction. Everyday something ends and something begins.

⎯⎯►◆◄⎯⎯

As the month of February ends, the planets Venus and Jupiter creep close to each other in the western sky. Saturn, modestly bright and yellowish white, rises above Jupiter and Venus, and Mercury dangles just above the horizon, a conjunction—a close alignment of astronomical bodies. Jupiter and Venus will not appear so close together for nearly a century.

This winter malaise—a malaise that spans all seasons for me—is certainly related to the human consciousness of time, to our sense of time passing and our passing with it. The philosopher E. M. Cioran alluded to this in an interview near the end of his life: "Boredom is connected naturally with time, with the horror of time, with the experience and consciousness of time. Those who are not aware of time do not become bored." My melancholy rises and falls with the rising and the falling of the planets in the western sky. I carefully observe and experience the passing of time, but for a moment now and then, I forget about time and stand in the dark cold night in sheer wonder of existence.

Along the Tracks of the Burlington Northern Railroad, Waterman

Abandoned Farm, Keslinger Road

Tree Grove in a Field of Corn Stubble, Keslinger Road

114

March

A half century ago, Aldo Leopold began his almanac's March entry by observing that "one swallow does not make a summer, but one skein of geese, cleaving the murk of a March thaw, is the spring." Flocks of geese were flying north over the sand country on their spring migration. Honking overhead and splashing down on marsh ponds, the geese were shaking "the last thought of winter out of the brittle cattails." Leopold measured the amplitude of spring by the number of geese that stopped to rest on the marsh pond. Wild geese have migrated twice yearly across the continent since the Pleistocene.

I hear the descendents of these geese, sometimes in the middle of the night, honking rhythmically as they fly high over my house. Yet through all the days of winter, I have been seeing another kind of Canada goose. This subspecies, larger than the high-flying migrant, spends the winter in the Midwest foraging around the open waters of suburban and corporate ponds, on golf courses and along drainage ditches, and on the lagoon within sight of my house. We are warned by the natural resource agencies that their numbers are growing dangerously high. We live daily with these resident geese, and I watch as they fly in circles low over my house. I must now look long and hard into the sky to trace the ancient pattern of the migrating geese.

The subspecies has found a home nearby, close to the ground. Meanwhile, the wild geese are flying home again. Mary Oliver has written about our relation to these geese in a poem titled "Wild Geese":

> Whoever you are, no matter how lonely,
> The world offers itself to your imagination,
> Calls to you like the wild geese, harsh and exciting—
> Over and over announcing your place
> In the family of things.

And I am coming home again to another spring.

—◆—

In the meantime, March storms have come in quick succession. We have had two heavy snowfalls within the week. Knee-deep in snow, with mind and spirit soaring, I have been photographing along the riverbanks and in the fields beside country roads.

Yesterday I fashioned myself after Claude Monet. Out-of-doors, I photographed the true effects of light on the snow. Monet, living with his family on the Normandy coast, wrote to a friend in December of 1868: "I go out into the country which is so beautiful here that I find the winter perhaps more agreeable than the summer, and naturally I am working all the time, and I believe that this year I am going to do some serious things." After a heavy snowfall, Monet painted the *Magpie,* depicting a fleeting moment of light and shadow and the sparse signs of life.

As I photograph the snow landscape, I think of the French impressionists—*en plein air, effets de neige.* In the white-shrouded fields, with the temperature "cold enough to split rocks," an art critic observed Monet at work: "We glimpsed a little heater, then an easel, then a gentleman swathed in three overcoats, with gloved hands, his face half frozen. It was M. Monet studying an aspect of the snow."

What is obscured in the summer heat is revealed to me in the black-and-white architecture of the winter landscape. As the sun shines on trees and branches and the snow glistens, I make my way with camera and tripod, looking from under my fur hat for just the right angle and the best light for the making of a photograph. I know abundance in the spareness of winter.

—◆—

When they could not paint out-of-doors—on rainy days or after too much coldness to the bone—the impressionists painted in their studios. Painting from earlier sketches, reworking canvases, painting portraits and nudes and still lifes, the impressionists continued their daily work. Pleasantly fatigued after four days of walking and photographing in the March snow, I take to house and home. Even indoors, this season I have the need to photograph, to still perhaps the pace of time, or to frame a composition that has the look of reality.

This is the time for my "still-life" work. Of course, I think of all of my photographs as still lifes. Whether I arrange objects for a particular effect or take what is given to me at the moment, the photograph is a composition constructed by me in the viewfinder of the camera. The result is a still life preserved on the film, an image of what once was but is no longer. Any work of art—especially a photograph, as Susan Sontag has reminded us—is a *momento mori.*

The term "still life" first appeared in the mid-seventeenth century to aid the inventory of paintings in Dutch households. Although the traditional still life portrays inanimate objects in relation to one another, the human presence is implicit in any still-life painting. A crumpled napkin, a musical instrument, a piece of fruit, a clock, a glass of wine, a loaf of bread, a book, a burning candle, perhaps a human skull, all these capture the fleeting moments of human existence. As art critic Anne Lowenthal writes, in the still life there is an "interplay between the animate and the inanimate, the moving and the motionless, the quick and the dead." The ordinary things of daily living are enhanced and elevated—and given meaning—in the still life. In the everyday world of routine and repetition, we know our salvation.

Thus the early definition of still life: *nature morte,* where the material objects of everyday life are isolated in repose. The earliest Western still lifes are by Dutch painters reminding us of human mortality: the *vanitas* paintings of Jan Davidsz de Heem, Willem Claesz Heda, Pieter van Steenwyck, and Jacques de Gheyn the Elder; paintings containing objects that symbolize the inevitability of death and the transience of vanity and earthly achievements. Not so much with repentance in mind, but with the thought of the impermanence of this human life, I make photographs. Still life on the border.

117

In the clear cold sky, the bright sun shines through bare trees and over rooftops and casts blue shadows on the hard surface of sparkling snow. The firm tracks of animals, both wild and tame, and the prints of the winged ones are read for the stories they tell. The mailman has left his tracks across the lawn as he has gone daily from house to house. I am pleasantly reminded of the words of the naturalist Ernest Thompson Seton: "To the young, oncoming naturalist, I would say: Never forget the trail, look ever for the track in the snow; it is the priceless, unimpeachable record of the creature's life and thought, in the oldest writing known on earth. Never forget the trail!"

All of us of the animal kingdom have the capacity for attention and observation. Our evolution, in fact, has been dependent upon the ability to observe what is happening around us. Even in flight, we give observation another chance. In her children's book of animal tracks, Betsy Bowen quotes Old Uncle of Ohiyesa on the example of the gray wolf: "You ought to follow the example of shunk-tokecha. Even when he is surprised and runs for his life, he will pause to take one more look at you before he enters his final retreat. So you must take a second look at everything you see." I will send a copy of *Tracks in the Wild* to my grandson before this month ends and the snow begins to melt.

⇒◆⇐

A month saved again by ordinariness. The mundane world filled with the wonder of daily living. A life lived and a life observed. My benediction for the month is from the epilogue of Zbigniew Herbert's *Still Life with Bridle:* "O holy ritual of everydayness, without you time is empty like a falsified inventory that corresponds to no real objects."

Still Life, Rolfe Road

East Lagoon in Winter, DeKalb

Kishwaukee River

April

The early morning sun of spring rises and shines through the east window of my upstairs bedroom—a sun that has greeted me for a good part of the century, a sun that I have known in other places in other circumstances.

In *The Man with the Little Dog,* Georges Simenon tells of a man in Paris waking up in the morning: "I have been awakened in the morning by the smell of coffee and the sound of my mother's footsteps in the kitchen, later by an alarm clock, then by the movements and the animal warmth of a woman's body. A baby's whimperings have aroused me from sleep, or the patter of a child's footsteps in the next room." Years can be marked—spring mornings can be recalled—by the directions of our lives.

—————⇒◆⇐—————

The *New York Times* gives the extended weather forecast for this Easter weekend: "Clusters of showers and thunderstorms will develop across parts of eastern Nebraska, Iowa, southern Minnesota and eventually Wisconsin as increasing moist winds from the south are lifted by the Nebraska low and its associated warm front." Temperatures will be in the upper sixties. The sun glows softly.

Meanwhile, in another part of the world, thousands of refugees flee across the border. A fog covers the land, and rain falls intermittently as a grandmother is carried in a blanket along a railroad track. Air strikes by stealth bombers continue, forgetting that we are all in this life together and that what we have in common is far greater than our differences.

—————⇒◆⇐—————

Whatever else we are doing in our lives, we are witnesses to our times, witnesses to all the joys and all the sorrows of being alive at this particular historical moment. As witnesses we may be moved by conscience to report what we have observed. An Armenian poet, known as Siamanto, writes of a German woman who witnessed a mass killing a century ago:

> This thing I'm telling you about,
> I saw with my own eyes.
> From my window of hell
> I clenched my teeth
> And watched the town of Bardez turn
> Into a heap of ashes.

Even in the quiet of a monastery, witness is being made. In *Boris Godunov,* Alexander Puskhin has the monk Primen speak of his witnessing to the history of czarist Russia. Writing by lamplight, Primen makes a final entry:

> One more, the final record, and my annals
> Are ended, and fulfilled the duty laid
> By God on me a sinner. Not in vain
> Hath God appointed me for many years
> A witness, teaching me the art of letters;
> A day will come when some laborious monk
> Will bring to light my zealous, nameless toil,
> Kindle, as I, his lamp, and from the parchment
> Shaking the dust of ages will transcribe
> My true narrations.

As the lines portend, someday the report will be found, and perhaps it will be of use and valued.

Sitting at my desk and hearing the reports on the radio of the latest atrocities, I hope in some way to make my own witness, even if that witness is simply a reverence for life or a few notes each day about living on the border at the end of the century. Nothing dramatic or special, just the attempt to live the best I can in this place and in these times.

——⟫•◦•⟪——

Only a few months ago I was in Paris visiting my daughter Anne—strolling the streets, exploring the apartments and nightly haunts of writers and artists, going deep into the catacombs to see millions of skeletons and skulls, and walking through the arcades of the nineteenth century. While in Paris, I found the word that has characterized my life for a long time: *flâneur.* A century and a half ago, Charles Baudelaire wrote about the flâneur:

> The crowd is his element, as the air is that of birds and water of fishes. His passion and his profession are to become one flesh with the crowd. For the perfect flâneur, for the passionate spectator, it is an immense joy to set up house in the heart of the multitude, amid the ebb and flow of movement, in the midst of the fugitive and the infinite. To be away from home and yet to feel oneself everywhere at home; to see the world, to be at the centre of the world, and yet to remain hidden from the world—such are a few of the slightest pleasures of those independent, passionate, impartial natures which the tongue can but clumsily define.

The flâneur is an enthusiastic observer—a kind of witness, I would say—and a lover of life who makes the whole world a family. Baudelaire continues, "We might liken him to a mirror as vast as the crowd itself; or to a kaleidoscope gifted with consciousness, responding to each one of its movements and reproducing the multiplicity of life and the flickering grace of all the elements of life." A lover of the universal life, beyond all boundaries and borders.

My little French dictionary is concise on the flâneur, even for today: "One who strolls the city streets leisurely, without destination or haste, abandoning himself to the fleeting impressions of the spectacle of the moment." And—relating to my own life in particular—I note an observation on the photographer as flâneur made by Susan Sontag in her book, *On Photography:* "The photographer is an armed version of the solitary walker reconnoitering, stalking, cruising the urban inferno, the voyeuristic stroller who discovers the city as a landscape of voluptous extremes." Whether searching for the extremes or finding simplicity in everyday life, I know that I am a flâneur, a witness to the wonder of life. Even when this human existence seems devoid of any inherent meaning, we make our daily rounds, we observe, and we wait. I hear Mimi singing to Rodolpho in Act III of *La Bohème:* "No one feels alone in April."

————⬥————

As Walter Benjamin, the German social critic, fled Paris in the spring of 1940, he carried a briefcase containing the manuscript of his study of the passages of Paris. For years he had been working on this project in the reading room of the Bibliothèque Nationale. He was fascinated—aesthetically and theoretically—by these nineteenth-century constructions of rational planning that promoted commodity capitalism: glass-roofed, marble-walled arcades or galleries with their elegant shop windows laden with food and drink, jewelry, and fine clothes and upper floors offering various pleasures for sale. These were mystical places where flâneurs participated in the modern spectacle, experiencing the transitory moment in the passageways of the city.

Along with two million fellow residents of Paris, Benjamin had to flee to the south of France when Hitler's army converged on the city. After spending the summer in Lourdes, he then traveled to Marseilles, hoping to obtain an emergency visa from the United States consulate. Unable to gather all the documents he needed, Benjamin and his companions decided to slip over the Spanish border. From Banyuls-sur-Mer, they crossed the Pyrenees. Impaired by his heart condition, Benjamin had to rest every ten minutes of walking. Exhausted and depressed, Benjamin took a hotel room in the small coastal town of Portbou. That night, he died in his room, taking his own life, despairing of being able to escape by train to Lisbon. His few possessions were confiscated and turned over to the local court, and eventually they were lost. His remains were probably interred in a common grave in the local cemetery.

In 1994, a monument was dedicated to Benjamin on the seaward side of the cemetery in Portbou. Cut into the cliff, stairs descend steeply to the rocks and sea below. Today's traveler confronts a glass plate at the end of the passageway. Engraved on the glass is a single quotation from the writings of Benjamin: "It is more arduous to honor the memory of the nameless than that of the renowned. Historical reconstruction is devoted to the memory of the nameless." The only way out of the monument is for visitors to retrace their steps above the rocks and the sea.

The flâneur at rest: dead, among the countless and nameless others who made history strolling the streets and passageways that lead to secret places. Lives lived often without aim or purpose, but lived in the center of things. For Benjamin, and for the many others, the crowded streets are places of daily renewal. Writing of Paris—and of strolling, idling, and *flânerie*—Hannah Arendt writes the following in her introduction to the life of Benjamin:

> The city has been the paradise of all those who need to chase after no livelihood, pursue no career, reach no goal—the paradise, then, of bohemians, and not only of artists and writers but all those who have gathered about them because they could not be integrated either politically—being homeless or stateless—or socially.

I am among those who need a Paris in their lives. In my imagination, I think of myself like Walter Benjamin, a daily flâneur. I listen now to Count Basie's rendition of "April in Paris": "One more once."

⋙◈⋘

My mother died yesterday. I was with her; she had waited through the night for us to come. She waited in the farmhouse where she had lived alone since my father died thirty years ago. I held her hand and cradled her head.

Someday life may seem to be right again. But for now, I cannot imagine a world without my mother. Surely nothing will ever be the same again.

Bedroom, Rolfe Road

Balcony View, Rue du Plâtre

128

Abandoned Farm with Jet Trail, Old State Road

May

I had expected a May of spring delights. Trips to the farm and walks through the marsh. Afternoons of sitting at the kitchen table with my mother, a gentle breeze rustling the lace curtains. A few words of encouragement and hope before heading south again. We would wave another goodbye.

But otherwise. I sit now with the diaries. I found the diaries in the middle drawer of the high bureau. I had learned of their existence a year ago, when my mother told me that she had kept diaries as a young girl. Her mother had given her the blank books to keep a record of her daily life.

A year ago I asked my mother if I might read the diaries, if I might take them home for the weekend. "Oh, you won't find anything of interest in them," she had said. "Nothing much happened in those days." She would have let me take them home if I had insisted, but I did not. "Some other time," she said.

My mother—Alice Marie Holloway—began keeping a diary in 1916 when she was nine years old. She made an entry every day for five years. "You have neither the time nor the inclination, possibly, to keep a full diary," begins the inscription at the front of one of the small volumes. It continues:

> Suppose, however, out of the multitude of matters that crowd each day, you jot down in a line or two those most worthy of remembrance. Such a book will be of the greatest value in after years. What a record of events, incidents, joys, sorrows, successes, failures, things accomplished, things attempted. This book is designed for just such a record.

A Borderland Almanac

It was 20 below zero. Alice Jordan froze her face going to school.
(Thursday, January 13, 1916)

Warmer. It snowed some. Mama played with colored dolls and blocks with me. Mama made me two little cakes and a pumpkin pie.
(Saturday, January 15, 1916)

Papa went to church and in the afternoon we went to Grandma's and we had popcorn. It was very cold.
(Sunday, January 16, 1916)

Did not go to school. Very windy. Mama and I played school.
(Monday, January 17, 1916)

Went to Elkhorn and bought a dish for mama and a handkerchief for papa and an eraser, tablet and composition book. Had dinner at the Hotel.
(Saturday, January 22, 1916)

Went to school. It rained. We got some things from Sears and Roebuck. I got some slippers and stockings for my doll. They were white. They were so pretty. On the slippers were the prettiest white bows.
(Monday, March 6, 1916)

I played out doors. Mama put a hen nest up for me. I did not get any eggs at night. We got some little pigs. One pig had 16 pigs. Two had 10 apiece.
(Saturday, March 11, 1916)

Went to school. We sawed wood. I got 1 egg. I got an invitation to Hazel McQuillen's birthday party. Mama got 25 eggs.
(Monday, March 20, 1916)

Your young words, your voice, your young life. Growing up on the farm north of Millard, attending the South Heart Prairie School, visiting your grandparents, traveling to church and to town, being cared for by your mother and father, playing with your dolls, gathering eggs from the hen's nest. The person that I would know as my mother, the mother that I would be with until the very end. And yesterday I placed flowers at your grave. A year ago this time, you and I together placed flowers on your own parents' graves.

For days I have been listening to Allen Ginsberg's reading of his kaddish for his mother. Yes, maybe we are as old as the universe and, yes, at the same time, "what came is gone forever every time." Done with this earthly existence. Eternity without day or night.

⚬

Hunted eggs all day. I got 2 eggs for myself and 30 for mama. Played in the mud with ma's boots on. Papa went to town. I got my Kodak.
(Saturday, March 25, 1916)

Went to school. Papa went to Whitewater. Someone broke the window playing antiover. Papa got some film for my camera.
(Tuesday, April 11, 1916)

Had a birthday party. There were 21 here (all girls). Each one brought me a present. Grandma came and helped mama with supper. I was 10 years old.
(Saturday, April 29, 1916)

I took my camera to school. Teacher showed me how to take a picture. Teacher took a picture of me. Jack (my cat) would not hold still so I could not take his picture. We went to Millard and back in the car. I wore my hat to school.
(Tuesday, May 4, 1916)

We had a short auto ride. Took Grandma's picture. I had the head ache all day. Papa and I went to the woods. I took a picture of mama and papa in the car. Papa took a picture of me at night. (Sunday, May 7, 1916)

Did not go to school. I was not sick. I was lazy. Papa painted some of the garage. Jack (is my cat) slept with me in the afternoon. I got up at 4:30 P.M. Papa painted the milkhouse. (Monday, May 8, 1916)

I am looking through the boxes of photographs, the boxes that I have labeled "Family." I am making prints of a photo I took of my mother on Thanksgiving Day two years ago to give to my daughters and to my brother's children. A lifetime of trying to stop time. Twenty years ago, my mother placed her camera in the bureau drawer and for the rest of her life took no more photographs.

How many times had I almost asked my mother about her understanding of the meaning of life? How many times had I nearly asked her about death and its meaning? At the last moment I withheld the questions for fear of disturbing her or intimating that I was anticipating her death. All along it was I who feared the questions. Likely my mother would have responded with something like "I don't know," or "You ask such impossible questions." "We live the best we can while we are here" was the philosophy of her life. Whether she feared death—or to what extent—I will never know. Certainly in her last hour she did not have the look in her eyes of wanting to go.

Two photographs my mother took in the spring of 1916, when she was learning how to use her new camera, still survive in a cardboard box: the one of her mother and father sitting in an automobile in the driveway of the farm and the one of her grandmother standing on the lawn in front of the house. These photographs remind us that what we see will change and finally pass away.

—————

Stayed home. Snowed all day.
(Tuesday, January 1, 1918)

Everyone got out and broke roads. No school. Beautiful day. Snow 4 feet deep in the road. Uncle Lloyd put cattle in the new barn.
(Monday, January 14, 1918)

Everyone moved with sleighs. Lots of ice and water. Went to school. Am knitting squares for Belgium blanket.
(Friday, March 1, 1918)

Went to Lyden to see the soldiers. 3,000 all on horses.
(Thursday, May 16, 1918)

Paper hanger was here. Papered the parlor and sitting room.
(Monday, May 20, 1918)

Had picnic. Passed in all studies with high standings. Will be in 7th grade next year. (Won 2 prizes).
(Friday, May 24, 1918)

Thrashed in the afternoon. Got 860 bushels of barley.
(Wednesday, August 21, 1918)

We went to Delavan to the picnic in Tilden's woods. A soldier that had been a prisoner in Germany 2 years spoke.
(Wednesday, August 28, 1918)

Had salt fish for dinner. (Drank water all the afternoon.) Mama and I picked ducks. Feathers all over.
(Thursday, October 24, 1918)

Went to school. Telegram came saying Germany had surrendered. We rang the school bell. The church bells rang in the towns. They rang for an hour. Everyone was excited.
(Thursday, November 7, 1918)

This report was not so. That the war was over. Went to school.
(Friday, November 8, 1918)

Report came that the war was over. (It is so this time.) Got word at 2 o'clock A.M. People celebrated all day. Went to Elkhorn at night.
(Monday, November 11, 1918)

Went to school. Went to town. Took my baby bed down.
(Tuesday, November 26, 1918)

The passing of an era, I have heard it said. My good friend from high-school days wrote to me the day after my mother died. After his words of comfort and support, he quoted a statement he had heard from a minister at Easter time many years ago: "To conquer death we merely have to die." I thought about that statement in the days before the funeral, its simple circularity.

The church was important to my mother's life. Growing up on the farm north of Millard, my mother attended church nearly every Sunday. She made certain that her two sons went to the Methodist Church in Delavan as they were growing up, too. For thirty years, all of her widowed years, she drove to church each Sunday morning—except in stormy weather or when in poor health. Yet outside of the social institution of the church, I never heard my mother speak of religion, not even to mention the word "God." Her concern was in doing the right thing. Doing unto others as you would have others do unto you. Theology was not an issue. She did tell me once that I was in her prayers.

I am fortunate to have lived near my mother during my own aging years. A friend with a similar blessing has suggested that we will forever be changed by the loss of our mothers. Another friend from afar, whose mother and father died a few months ago, tells me that his own life has changed in unanticipated ways since the deaths of his parents. He says that he realizes now "that life is not practice." We are not preparing for anything; life is what we are doing at the moment. "Everything will work out because it is working out." A loosening unto the world. My mother would have agreed.

—⊳—

Grandma and Grandpa came down to dinner. We had duck and ice cream. Was a little colder at night. I have had a cough all day.
(Wednesday, January 1, 1919)

Went to school. At night went to Woodmen banquet. Played games after supper. They danced. Got home about half past twelve.
(Wednesday, February 12, 1919)

Was my birthday. Got a pair of silk gloves and silk stockings from mama and a box of candy from papa.
(Tuesday, April 29, 1919)

Went to Sunday School in the morning. At night went up to Grandma's. Took her for a little ride.
(Sunday, June 1, 1919)

Ma and pa went to Janesville after a pony. Bought Trixy. Ma drove her home. Trixy is 4 years old.
(Friday, July 25, 1919)

Papa went to mill. Drove Trixy for the first time alone.
(Tuesday, July 29, 1919)

Went to Parker's hog sale at Janesville. I got a new camera. Mama got a new skirt and waist.
(Tuesday, August 19, 1919)

Cooler today. School at Millard went better. Drove Trixy.
(Tuesday, September 9, 1919)

Went up to Grandma's. Stayed up there all night.
(Saturday, September 27, 1919)

Went to school. Grandma died in the morning. Rained.
(Tuesday, September 30, 1919)

We went to the funeral. Rev. Clemons preached. Clear.
(Friday, October 2, 1919)

Cold. We did not go to church. Grandpa came down to supper. November has been cold with lots of rain. Up to now I have driven to school every day and put Trixy in Patchen's barn.
(Monday, November 30, 1919)

The day before the funeral, Laura and I drove up to the farm. We sat for a while in the house, then walked the farm and took a few photographs. We ended our wandering at the old place where my great-grandparents had built their house. Later we drove south over the border and toward home.

My mother was well remembered the next afternoon at the United Methodist Church of Delavan. All of our relatives and neighbors and friends were there to celebrate "A Liturgy of Death and Resurrection." Pastor Johnson delivered a fitting and much-appreciated eulogy. The recessional was accompanied by an Irish tune, "Be Thou My Vision."

We drove through the streets of Delavan to the Spring Grove Cemetery where the grave site already held the remains of my father. As the final scriptures and prayers were read, a gentle rain began to fall. A reception and lunch served by the Methodist women brought us back to the church. Tonight I am listening to a new rendition of the bluegrass song "Forever Blue": "I can't get over you—forever blue."

>–<

The last year my mother kept a diary was 1920. She was then fourteen. Her own mother would die in September of the following year. I always knew that my mother missed her mother every day for the rest of her life.

> *We and Uncle Lloyd and Aunt Elsie and Grandpa went to Uncle Frank's to dinner. Snowed and drifted the night before. 18 below. We were going sleigh riding at night, but it was too cold.*
> *(Thursday, January 1, 1920)*

> *Elkhorn schools closed until after the flu. Ma and pa's wedding day.*
> *(Tuesday, February 3, 1920)*

> *Went to school. Walked home. Papa went to Delavan and brought home a Victrola.*
> *(Friday, February 20, 1920)*

138

Easter. Went to church. Snowed a little. Cold at night. Went up to Aunt Elsie's at night.
(Sunday, April 4, 1920)

School picnic at Turtle Lake. Got my diploma and standings. Was valedictorian of my class.
(Saturday, June 4, 1920)

Rained. Papa went to town with oats. An aeroplane went over.
(Thursday, June 17, 1920)

Nice day. Picked gooseberries and currents. I made some current jam.
(Friday, July 9, 1920)

Fine day. We all went to Racine. Aunt Rachel went with us. In the afternoon went to the shore of
Lake Michigan. At night went to a vaudeville.
(Saturday, August 7, 1920)

I began high school at Elkhorn. Nice day.
(Monday, September 13, 1920)

Moved down to Millard.
(Wednesday, November 10, 1920)

Went up to Uncle Lloyd's. Mrs. Uglow and Myrtle and Elva were there. Had a swell dinner. Stayed
to supper. Had oysters.
(Saturday, December 25, 1920)

I was not ready, preparing for the funeral, to be told by the clergy that although we mourn, we mourn with hope (the hope of eternal life.) The day after the funeral, I went to the basement, found my copy of W. H. Auden's *Collected Poems,* and turned to the poem popularized in the movie *Four Weddings and a Funeral.* One stanza of this poem conveys utter hopelessness and despair:

> The stars are not wanted now: put out every one;
> Pack up the moon and dismantle the sun;
> Pour away the ocean and sweep up the wood;
> For nothing now can ever come to any good.

Like my mother, I am more uplifted—and able to go on—when I am facing the reality of the moment. Eventually, I am certain, there will be hope. For now, I am thankful, and I know my good fortune.

⋙◆⋘

My mother, at least in the later years, gave me little direct advice on how to live my life, but I knew from the example of her life, from the way she had lived, that life's instructions were clear: Be kind, be thoughtful, be helpful whenever you can.

These days I find myself reciting the ending she gave to all the letters and the many notes of thanks that she wrote to me. These letters and notes are in a wooden box on the top shelf of my closet. Someday I will get them down again, whenever I need to be reminded of her voice—of her good life. In the meantime, the departing words of each letter will suffice, unceasingly: *As ever, Mom.*

House at the Farm

Dining-room Window with Plants

Bedroom

June

The words of a character from Samuel Beckett: "I'll never know, in the silence you don't know, you must go on, I can't go on, I'll go on." High over the Atlantic, the jet plane takes me to Paris to see Anne, to spend time, to go on.

Passing through French Customs, I have nothing to declare. All I am carrying of value is my loss. Another summer of possibility. There have been other summers in Paris when one life seemed to be ending and another beginning. With luck, or intention, there may be some spiritual development. Perhaps this is what is meant by the triumph of life over death. As always, everything of spiritual significance comes out of the fabric of everyday life.

Welcome to Paris. The Blue Line takes me directly to the Metro station Châtelet/Les Halles. Anne is waiting for me on the platform. We walk past the Pompidou Centre and into the Marais. Up the six fights of stairs of the apartment building on rue du Plâtre, and I am in my Paris room.

⇒◆⇐

I have brought my large camera to photograph the galleries, the passages, and the arcades. I spend a day in the Gallerie Vivienne, beside the Bibliothèque Nationale, photographing. I imagine Walter Benjamin strolling and looking into shop windows during his breaks from working in the library. Midday light flows through the glass of the high vaulted roof. Anne takes my picture standing in the Place des Petits Pères. Jean Paul Sartre, in the form of a statue, walks briskly through the gardens of the Bibliothèque Nationale. Leisurely, we sit and have a glass of beer in a nearby café.

⇒◆⇐

I have located the Paris residences of Samuel Beckett. For years after the war, he lived at number 6, rue des Favorites, just off the rue de Vaugirard in the fifteenth *arrondissement,* not far from his favorite area, Montparnasse. In an apartment on the seventh floor, on a street of factories and workshops, Beckett would write his sparse works, pondering the nature of reality and our tenuous grip on it. The first-person monologue would cut away any pretense of knowability or omnipotence.

Over the years, I have learned much about the loose and uncertain nature of reality from Beckett. I am silent much of the time, but finally I cannot keep from speaking and writing the words. And, with Beckett, I am always waiting for Godot. Even my own existence is often in doubt.

In the 1960s, Beckett and his wife, Suzanne, moved into a new and much larger apartment at 38, boulevard Saint-Jacques. It is located on a busy and noisy modern thoroughfare in the fourteenth arrondissement, within walking distance of the boulevard du Montparnasse. The apartment building still looks smart and new, with its façade of plate-glass windows. Large shade trees line the boulevard. As he sat at his desk, Beckett would wave from the rear window of the apartment to inmates in the prison behind the apartment building. He would entertain visitors in the hotel on the other side of the boulevard.

Eventually, at the end of the 1980s, Beckett moved to an old people's home, Tiers Temps, also in the fourteenth arrondissement. The window of his room overlooked a courtyard that contained a single tree. He would sit at his small writing table under the window in monastic simplicity, always a bottle of Irish whiskey at hand for himself and his visitors.

One of Beckett's last visitors, a poet, asked him if he had found much of the journey worthwhile. "Precious little," he replied. But with more Irish whiskey and a certain mellowness, Beckett suddenly began to sing a Church of Ireland hymn:

> Now the day is over,
> Night is drawing nigh,
> Shadows of the evening
> Steal across the sky.

Nothing is certain, and consolations are few.

On a warm evening, before darkness, we walk the boulevard Saint-Jacques. We pause in front of the apartment building at number 38, take a photograph in the low light, utter a few words of appreciation, and move on to the Butte aux Cailles. We have a fine dinner to celebrate my sixty-fifth birthday at a restaurant run by the workers' cooperative.

———◆———

Our train speeds toward Poitiers, an hour and a half southwest of Gare Montparnasse. Large, tall cumulus clouds float above the green fields. Farms, villages, and grain elevators beside the tracks pass by. We are on our way to a conference—titled La Révolte—on the life and work of Albert Camus. I will be on the periphery as Anne participates in the sessions. There are streets to roam in this ancient city, with its Romanesque churches and cathedrals and palaces from the time of Henry II and Eleanor of Aquitaine. I will not miss the exhibition of Hiroshige prints at the Musée Saint-Croix, and I will look longing once again at Camille Claudel's bronze statue, *La Valse.*

Between sessions at the conference, Anne and I talk about Camus. My walks through the city, especially my visits to the churches, confirm Camus's great and courageous message: the absurdity of most social and moral traditions. The heroes in the novels of Camus refuse to surrender to convention and self-deceit. Meursault, in *The Stranger,* refuses to compromise with hypocrisy. Through honesty and revolt he is liberated, a person true to existential being. Amid the indifference of a world devoid of God, the value of living in the present moment is affirmed.

In the brief time since my mother's death, I too am trying to face the absurdity of the end of her life. A positive revolt in Poitiers is to affirm life—our lives and my mother's life—as it is lived in this world. Near the end of the conference, Anne introduces me to a professor of English from India, who gives us a copy of the paper he had presented earlier that day. Concluding the paper, he quotes Tolstoy in support of the essential Camus: "All of us must discover all the futilities of life in order to come back to life itself."

Back in Paris, the night before I am to fly home, we gather with friends at a Tunisian restaurant. Tagine dishes are served. High in the Belleville of Paris, along the narrow street, sitting around the dinner table out-of-doors, night comes slowly. In the sky above and beyond appear the stars and planets of our universe. We may not know the world ultimately, but we live wondrously in it daily.

The next afternoon I sit in the Charles de Gaulle airport holding the lunch that Anne has packed for me. On the long flight home from Paris to Chicago, I make no attempt to read or to write or to think about much at all. I catch the conclusion of *You've Got Mail,* the westbound flight's feature film. Meg Ryan's character joyfully exclaims to Tom Hanks's character, after establishing their true identities, "I wanted it to be you." Finally, we are recognized for who we really are.

Crop Duster, Annie Glidden Road

Guest Room, Rue du Plâtre

Flâneur, Galerie Vivienne

July

The warm bright mornings of July. I am walking through an emerging woodland on a hill that once was the grazing ground for a herd of Holstein and Jersey cows. It is now the farm my brother and I co-own, but it is always the farm of those who preceded us—our parents, grandparents, and great-grandparents. And I know that I am part of the natural succession of plants and animals on the hillside. The closely cut, grazed grasses have given way to hundreds of trees. Oaks and hickories seeded in the ground by squirrels and crows and songbirds now stand tall and dense. Nature takes back what was hers all along. We are all squatters, including the Potawatomi who once summered here. We are on the land for a time, and then to it we return.

We thus cherish the world, living fully in the transience of reality, fascinated and charmed by its traces and reflections. Graced in reverie, I walk through the woods, the marshland, and the planted fields of this much-loved farm. All of nature, including this rotting tree trunk on which I rest, is in the process of becoming something else.

I am a stroller in these woods. This has been my form of participation in the world—sauntering from morning to night. Whether on the streets of a city or in the thickness of the woods, I have attended to the details of this everyday life. Roaming, observing, and occasionally noting in my journal the mystery of this life. Fragments have been gathered—in writings and in photographs—from a world that can never be grasped wholly.

My life, it seems, has been one of actively observing the world. And such was the life of Henry David Thoreau. At the beginning of his account of going to live in the woods beside Walden Pond, Thoreau wrote, "For many years I was self-appointed inspector of snow storms and rain storms, and did my duty faithfully." For years, Thoreau has been an inspiration and a guide for my own life. He found a universe within himself and on the borders of the landscape close to home. Thoreau was fully employed in the daily observations and reflections that he made in his journal.

This summer I think especially about Thoreau's visit to the Midwest. Just a few miles north of where I live, Thoreau passed on a train speeding from Chicago to a station near the Mississippi on the Illinois and Wisconsin border. Each time I drive north to the farm and cross the tracks on Annie Glidden Road, I think of Thoreau sitting in the coach car and looking out of the window at a countryside far from his New England home. On an early summer morning in 1861, he returned home on these tracks for the last summer of his life.

⟫⬥⟪

Thoreau's feats of hiking and outdoor living were more the result of will and desire than physical constitution. For years he suffered the effects of tuberculosis. Finally in 1861, the year before he died, his doctor advised him to seek a change of climate. The doctor suggested that he take a long journey to the West Indies or the south of France or the Mississippi Valley. Perhaps because of the lower cost of a trip to the Midwest or because of his interest in American flora and fauna, Thoreau decided to travel to Minnesota. The journey began from Concord on the 11th of May and ended when he returned home on the 10th of July.

After stopping at Niagara Falls and Detroit for a few days, Thoreau and his traveling companion, Horace Mann, Jr., a student of botany, reached Chicago on the 21st of May. Resting for a couple of days at the Metropolitan House, visiting a Unitarian minister, they bought tickets for the train trip to St. Paul. Thoreau saw the prairie for the first time as the train rolled across northern Illinois to Dunleith. From the port on the Mississippi, Thoreau and Mann went up the river by boat, stopping along the way at Prairie du Chien. From their room in St. Paul, Mann wrote a letter to his mother, saying that Mr. Thoreau "is doing very well now and I think will be a great deal better before long."

Thoreau's journal of the trip is devoted mainly to natural history. He went to geological and botanical museums, talked to naturalists, read books and reports, gathered and identified many specimens, and searched eagerly for a wild crab apple tree. He observed and noted the many species of birds and animals—wild pigeons in enormous flocks, turkey buzzards and herons, kingfishers and jays, swallows, ducks, and turtles. He showed little interest in frontier life and was embarrassed by a Sioux Indian dance staged in Redwood for the party of travelers.

At the end of June, Thoreau was ready to return home. He and Mann left Minnesota on the 26th for Prairie du Chien. They then took the train to Milwaukee, passing through Madison at 1:30 in the afternoon. They reached Concord the second week of July, traveling by way of Mackinaw City, Toronto, Ogdensburg, Vermont, and New Hampshire.

The excursion totaled 3,500 miles, the longest trip Thoreau had ever made. Even at that, Thoreau had cut the trip short by a month or more, possibly because of homesickness and certainly because of the continuing illness in his chest. Some years ago, a literary commentator, John T. Flanagan, suggested another reason for Thoreau's early return: "Possibly also he realized that there was no cure for him, and he desired to spend his final lingering days in the setting endeared to him by nature and man. In any event, he never left home again." Becoming weaker during the winter, Thoreau died on May 6, 1862. Flanagan ends his commentary: "It is indeed a heavy loss that Thoreau did not live to do for the woods of Minnesota and the land of the Sioux what he had already done for Concord and for Maine."

Near the end, a friend had asked Thoreau how the opposite shore appeared to him. Thoreau answered, summing up the way he had lived his whole life, "One world at a time." In a last letter, Thoreau observed the effects of the night's rain on the gravel of the railroad causeway. Thoreau concluded the letter: "All this is perfectly distinct to an observant eye, and yet could easily pass unnoticed by most. Thus each wind is self-registering." Earlier he had noted that each life is self-registering. We make our observations, take a few notes, and pass on.

The Marsh on the Farm

154

Illinois Central Tracks at Annie Glidden Road

Grain Elevator, Highway 64 and Five Points Road

August

I am sitting this morning at the dining-room table in the farmhouse, the hottest week of the summer. I have decided to spend a few days in the house. Yesterday and this morning—without great intent or planning—I cleaned out some drawers, washed woodwork, rearranged dishes, removed dead flies and moths from the windowsills, and trimmed the lower branches of the spruce that rubs against the bedroom on the north side of the house. The temperature will rise to the upper nineties today. Last night, in the hot and humid bedroom, I rested uncomfortably and dreamed fitfully.

For awhile, if not forever, this house will belong to another time and to my mother and father who built it the year they were married. The tall Chinese elms that they planted to shade the house on summer days continue to do so. This is the homeplace, and it will be as much of home as I will ever know.

In this summer's heat and haze, I remember the August days of fifty years ago and more. The second cutting of hay would be mowed and dried in the sun, loaded onto the wagon, and pulled to the barn. The two-pronged fork would be plunged into the top of the load, and one by one, large clumps of hay would be hoisted to the top of the barn. The team of sweating horses would pull the long rope over the ground carrying the fork of hay to its destination in the mow. The hay would be released, falling to its place for winter feed. The fork would be pulled back by hand and another forkload would be prepared. The empty wagon would be driven back to the field for another load of hay. Sometimes we would rest with a glass of ice-water under the oak in the front yard.

At the end of August, the threshing machine was pulled into the oat field and placed south of the barn. Farm neighbors came with their wagons drawn by teams of horses. The threshing crew would stop working at noon. The power belt from the tractor would be released and the threshing machine would fall silent. The horses would be placed in the shade under the elms and given water and feed. In the backyard, each man washed his face and hands

157

in the white enamel pan that rested in the wrought-iron stand. Fresh towels hung on each stand.

After a morning of cooking, my mother and the neighbor women served the noon meal on the back porch at a table as wide as the porch itself. Mashed potatoes were passed, meat loaf and gravy, green peas, and hot apple pie with chunks of cheddar cheese for dessert. My mother and her friends would receive compliments from the well-fed crew. Some of the men would wander off to complete the hour with a short nap under the elms.

At night we would go about the necessary chores in the hot barn. The cows were milked and released to the pasture. The tired horses rested in their stalls. I can still smell the steam rising from the harnesses that hung on the wall beside the stalls. We all wondered if one night's rest would be enough for the beginning of another day. But, for the moment, we could not imagine another life, nor did we care to.

And I am still here on this farm. There have been other places and other times, of course. Last night I slept in the room that was my bedroom sixty-five years ago. Today I write at the table that was here at my beginning.

I returned to the Midwest to be near this place several years ago in my search for home. I no longer search it, realizing that the goal is an impossible one. I really do not want to reach home, for I know now that home is attainable only in the ending, for which I am not prepared and for which I have no desire. The realization came to me earlier this week as I was reading a poem I had recorded in a journal some time ago and had forgotten. The lines are from the eighth-century Chinese poet Li Po:

> We the living, we're passing travelers:
> It's in death alone that we return home.

Barn Interior

Granary

Front Porch

September

The signs of a new season are beginning to appear. Gone are the wrens from their nest in the backyard. The ferns are dying and falling to the ground. This summer's heron no longer wades in the shallow waters of the lagoon. The drying leaves of the tall corn now blow in the wind. Cooling water laps against the dead trees protruding from the lake south of town. School buses crowd the roads in the afternoon. Tractors and combines are about to drive into the night. Waves of soybean dust will pass over the headlights of the great machines as they move through the fields. The prairie is being harvested.

Grain elevators will soon be filled. Vapors will rise out of vents as shelled corn dries in the night. Trucks are beginning to unload the harvest at the Shabbona Grain Company, named for the chief of the Potawatomi who once lived nearby. My own harvest for the season will be less tangible, as Henry David Thoreau understood as well: "The true harvest of my daily life is somewhat as intangible and indescribable as the tints of morning or evening. It is a little stardust caught, a segment of the rainbow which I have clutched." A photograph now and then, a few notes from the field, and a life passing with some intention each day.

—⇒◆⇐—

Each day I travel in some way—by car or on foot—the roads and byways of this county in northern Illinois. This is the landscape to which I returned after years of traveling in other places. It is a landscape of transcendent quality, having to do with the line of the horizon, the way the sky meets the land, the drift of the clouds over the fields and towns, the way the sun is reflected on the weathered barn.

Photographing the landscape, I have discovered the importance of watching all things as they rise and pass away, of seeing things as they really are. Experiencing the landscape in silence,

162

with bare attention, I become aware of the absolute wholeness of the world, of the reality beyond words. Everything of which I am part is immeasurable and mysterious.

⧯

Although life was harsh for John Muir as he grew up on the farm near Portage, Wisconsin, he knew the beauty of the place. Eventually he would write, "We all dwell in a house of one room—the world with the firmament for its roof—and are sailing the celestial spaces without leaving any track."

Now the power lines stretch from the Mississippi River to Chicago, cutting through the farm fields south of DeKalb. Suburbs and industrial parks sprawl over the landscape west of Chicago. New housing developments are filling the fields. And yet, as John Muir reminded us, this too will pass. When this landscape of farms, power lines, industrial parks, and houses is gone, the earth and the firmament will remain. Our true nature, outside of the discourse of the mind, is in a celestial space beyond the borderland, in a cosmos that stretches beyond the imagination. For the time being, this borderland of ours is everything.

On Waterman Road

164

Corn Harvest, Highway 30 Overpass

Shabbona Lake

October

October mornings follow nights of frost. The few remaining leaves on the trees shake against the wind. The vacant, abandoned house at the edge of town stands in ruins. Lines from Shakespeare speak of the season:

> That time of year thou mayst in me behold
> When yellow leaves, or none, or few, do hang
> Upon those boughs which shake against the cold,
> Bare ruined choirs where late the sweet birds sang.

Here now in this place is a sense sublime, an awareness of the union of past and present in the active forces of nature. The meditative act of photographing is my daily practice. Earth and sky are joined, too, in a sense of the sublime. As it was for the romantic poets and the transcendentalists, the sacred and the mundane are joined in everyday existence. In the words of William Wordsworth:

> And I have felt
> A presence that disturbs me with the joy
> Of elevated thoughts; a sense sublime.

The spiritual eye of the photographer beholds a landscape and becomes one with the world.

All seems eternal—to use that most transcendent of words—when we see a landscape in the silence of the moment, when we allow ourselves to be struck by wonder. The eternal is known concretely when we are present without thought of past or future, when we are unbounded by time. Wittgenstein writes in his *Tractatus Logico-Philosophicus,* "If we take eternity to mean not infinite temporal duration, but timelessness, the eternal life belongs to those who live in the present."

⟞⟞◆⟝⟝

At the end of his years, late in the seventeenth century, the poet Bashō walked the roads of northern Japan. He sold his house in Edo prior to his departure, not expecting to return from his wanderings. He took to the open road in the spirit of Buddha: life itself is a journey, a journey into eternity.

Along the way, Bashō was greeted by merchants, peasants, and monks. He rested and worshipped at Buddhist and Shinto shrines. He kept a journal of his travels and wrote haiku poems. In his journal he wrote that "those who steer a boat across the sea, or drive a horse over the earth till they succumb to the weight of years, spend every moment of their lives traveling."

For Bashō, and for all who travel with him, the journey is life itself. In all that will perish, we seek a vision of eternity. Finally, in the Zen sense, we "return to original mind"—our connection to all that exists. Eternity is in the interdependence of all things, arising and falling away. Our spiritual growth is in this realization.

⟞⟞◆⟝⟝

Jeremiah foretold the destruction of Jerusalem. On a recent visit to the Rijksmuseum in Amsterdam, I stood in front of the seventeenth-century painting that Rembrandt had made of Jeremiah lamenting the destruction of Jerusalem, and I realized, in addition to noting the destruction wrought by Nebuchadnezzar's troops, that if I had been Rembrandt I would have died two years ago.

In the evening, in the center of Amsterdam, I happen upon a demonstration for East Timor's independence from Indonesia. The songwriter and singer Daniel Sahuleka, from one of the Indonesian islands, sings, "Sometimes I wonder if I am going to make it home again." Despite the horrors of the latest events, I still feel the joy and the wonder of being part of this larger world. A witness to the times.

House in Ruins, Irene Road

Grain Elevator and Village Pizza, Malta

Reguliersgracht, Amsterdam

November

At the upper end of my street, one enters the grounds of the Ellwood House, passing the nineteenth-century mansion and into a grove of trees, the woods. And beyond the woods is the community cemetery with its tall oaks rising above the gravestones. In other seasons, I have walked through these wooded grounds in search of wildflowers and the three-leafed trillium. This season I find the remnants—dry stems, fallen leaves, and decaying matter—just another phase of this natural world of which we are an intimate part.

What lives and what dies? Death appears as the source of life this late season. With signs of renewal, the lessons of ecology, the dharma: life and death are interdependent. Life and death do not exist without each other. Where is the line between the living fungus and the rotting wood that nourishes it? All of this world exists because of death and decay. A line this day from one of Wendell Berry's *Sabbaths* poems: "Unmaking makes the world."

Death is a human conception; only the conditioned mind would call the leaf dead that is falling from the tree today. The leaf has spent the summer filling the tree with life. The energy of the leaf is in the growth of the tree. The leaf that falls is but an artifact. Life is elsewhere. No death on this day.

———⊰◆⊱———

With every arrival there is a departure, with every departure an arrival. Each time we travel—even in the wanderings of a single day—we are reminded of the ultimate meaning of travel, of coming and going, of leaving and returning, a reminder that there is no life without death, no death without life. We die simply because we have lived. Death is the price we pay for life, a return to where we were before we were born. We give life for the making of life. The universe favors life.

Still, we suffer a lifetime with thoughts of death, with the passing of those we love, and with fears about our own impending deaths. The oneness of life and death is intellectually true, but the fact and the thought are not enough to sooth the suffering. From our human, immediate perspective, death is death and little more. We finally turn to the comforts offered by one religion or another. Such is our human condition.

———◆———

I have been reading some of the letters that my mother saved in the drawers of the desk and the buffet, letters I wrote to my mother and father when I was in college and those I wrote while traveling in Europe in the 1960s. I had sent them when I was young, when all things were new, when I was leaving the farm and finding my way. And when I was still missing home.

I also found notes and clippings my mother saved over the years. A Bible kept on the table beside her chair in the living room contained pages torn from religious publications. Bookmarks were placed at Psalm 119, 2 Chronicles, and Paul's Epistle to the Romans. A page from the *Upper Room* begins with Isaiah 30:15, "In quietness and in trust shall be your strength." Another page opens with 1 John 3:11, the message we have heard from the beginning, that we should "love one another," and this quotation from a Methodist theologian:

> A true contemplative seeks and recognizes the presence of God in the normal activities of life, especially in interaction with others. In beauty, in nature, in the innocence of children, in the working out of justice in history, in countless ways we discern the presence of God. This kind of discernment begins to come to us when we have trained and conditioned ourselves to be open to the presence of God.

Another clipping, saved from the *Reader's Digest,* ends with an observation that could just as well have been written for my mother: "What you are when nobody's looking is what you really are." My mother's religious life was in her deeds. The words behind the deeds were placed between the pages of the books she kept for herself—and in her own heart and soul. Alone in the farmhouse for those many years, my mother lived as a contemplative, a woman with an active life grounded in quietness and solitude.

Yet her life had always extended to the larger world. She was informed about world events and concerned about suffering in the world. In the Bible beside her chair was a card containing the Maryknoll "World Peace Prayer":

> Lead me from death to life,
>   from falsehood to truth,
> Lead me from despair to hope,
>   from fear to trust,
> Lead me from hate to love,
>   from war to peace,
> Let peace fill our hearts,
>   our world, our universe.

Tree Trunk and Fungi, Ellwood House

Back Bedroom

Tracks in Sky and Snow, Annie Glidden Road

December

There is nothing like a millennium to make one aware of time—of the passing of time. This is not the end of just another year, but the end of a millennium and the coming of a new one. The transition, of course, does not actually occur until the year 2001, but most of us are eager to recognize the last midnight of 1999 as an extraordinary turning point. These are the last days of all we have known of the twentieth century. We are making ourselves ready in anticipation of the future.

I am now aware—along with multitudes of fellow humans on this planet—that one lifetime in a century is not enough. I am several beings living within the confines of a single lifetime. Many existences are needed to fulfill the possibilities of one's total being. Making the best of the one life I have in this world, I am finding that as I grow older I am indeed entering a larger world. A new millennium opens us to a world beyond the borders of time and place.

—————⊰◆⊱—————

A gentle snow falls these last days of the century. Snow covers the prairie fields and settles on tree trunks in wooded groves. Rivers bend between moist banks laced with freshly fallen snow. I am reminded of the closing passages of James Joyce's story, "The Dead." As Gabriel contemplates crooked crosses and headstones, "his soul swooned slowly as he heard the snow falling faintly through the universe and faintly falling, like the descent of their last end, upon all the living and the dead."

South of town, I visit the grove now called the Chief Shabbona Forest Preserve. Snow covers the trunks and branches of fallen oaks. Once the chief of the Potawatomi made a home here. Later, after the grove had been seized in questionable land dealings, he would be seen on his black-and-white pony, an aged rider moving along the river banks and across the prairies of northern Illinois, wife and grandchildren in the wagon. He painted his face black after advising

Black Hawk to make peace. Armies of settlers, he had said, are without number, like the sands on the seashore. Ruin will follow all who go to war. Rolled up in a blanket, Chief Shabbona slept out the cold nights.

Great fallen trees in the cover of snow this gentle day. Fields of weathered corn grazed by deer surround the grove. I wait, and watch, as the night approaches.

—————

How many times must we be instructed on the source and the reality of this existence? Rainer Maria Rilke, in his thirteenth sonnet to Orpheus, informs us about our beginnings in a great void:

> Be—and yet know the great void where all things begin,
> the infinite source of our inmost vibration,
> so that, this once, you may give it your perfect assent.

As old as the Vedic hymns is the habit of the human spirit to pose a duality. Nearly all cults and religions depend upon a separation between this life and some other world beyond everyday existence, almost as if we humans needed to be strangers to the world in order to feel deeply or to entertain the mystery of life, as if we needed to imagine that we really belong to some other place, that the present is not enough. Out of such needs gods are created. But is there not another way? The way beyond dualism, the way of oneness? There is no transcendence apart from this life. This life itself is the measure and source of all value. The sublime is in the wonder of daily life rather than in the reaching for something of another world. No myth-making, no God-making, but affirmation of this life.

And where does this world come from? What is the source of our being? Let us call it the void. Out of the void we have come, out of non-being, and to the void we return. Birth is but a manifestation of non-being. Death is a return to our non-being, beyond knowing, to the great void. We are here, completely and sublimely, when we merely let go to the moment. The way is very simple.

On the other side of town, there is a stand of white pine trees growing on the flood plain beside the Kishwaukee River. I walk into the woods on a cold and snowy day. A silence, a void, the source of our being. The practice of just letting go.

⟞⟊⟞

Many times on these winter days at the end of this millennium, I think of the lines from the diary of Dag Hammarskjöld:

> The light died in the low clouds. Falling snow drank in the dusk. Shrouded in silence the branches wrapped me in their peace. When the boundaries were erased, once again the wonder: that I exist.

Existence takes precedence. We begin with the wonder that anything at all exists, ourselves included. Existence is a mystery that is entertained in our daily lives. We approach the mystery not by reasoned thought and argumentation, but by experience. Existentialists and mystics, our method is meditative, a meditation on everyday experience.

There is the initial encounter. A crisis, perhaps. A stage of life. Suffering. Doubt. Joy. Illness. Time running out. Finally a sense of oneness. All these I now experience. I am called. In my notebook I write that my belief is in what I love.

I will watch closely, participate, experience the mystery. Make a visual record with my camera. Keep a pen and writing pad at hand, remembering that the goal is always beyond the material: compassion, love, union with all that exists. Once again the wonder.

Elm and Mulberry, Ellwood House

Chief Shabbona Forest Preserve

Grove of White Pines, DeKalb

184

Bibliography

Bibliography

Arendt, Hannah. "Walter Benjamin: 1892–1940." Introduction. *Illuminations,* by Walter Benjamin. Ed. Hannah Arendt. 1–55. New York: Schocken Books, 1969.

Auden, W. H. *Collected Poems.* Ed. Edward Mendelson. New York: Vintage, 1991.

Barthes, Roland. *Camera Lucida: Reflections on Photography.* Trans. Richard Howard. New York: Hill and Wang, 1981.

Bashō [Matsuo Bashō]. *The Narrow Road to the Deep North and Other Travel Essays.* Trans. Nobuyuki Yuasa. New York: Penguin, 1966.

Baudelaire, Charles. *The Painter of Modern Life.* Trans. Jonathan Mayne. London: Rhaidon, 1964.

Beckett, Samuel. *I Can't Go On, I'll Go On.* Ed. Richard Seaver. New York: Grove Press, 1976.

Beckett, Samuel. *Stories and Texts for Nothing.* Trans. Richard Seaver. New York: Grove Press, 1970.

Benjamin, Walter. "On Some Motifs in Baudelaire." *Illuminations.* Ed. Hannah Arendt. 155–200. New York: Schocken Books, 1969.

Benjamin, Walter. "Paris, Capital of the Nineteenth Century." *Reflections.* Ed. Peter Demetz. 146–62. New York: Schocken Books, 1986.

Berger, John, and Jean Mohr. *A Fortunate Man.* New York: Pantheon Books, 1967.

Bernanos, Georges. *The Diary of a Country Priest.* 1937. Trans. Pamela Morris. New York: Carroll and Greb Publishers, 1983.

Berry, Wendell. *Sabbaths.* San Francisco: North Point Press, 1987.

Bly, Robert. *Silence in the Snowy Fields.* Middletown, Conn.: Wesleyan University Press, 1962.

Bowen, Betsy. *Tracks in the Wild.* Boston: Houghton Mifflin, 1998.

Bowles, Paul. *Days: Tangier Journal, 1987–1989.* New York: Ecco Press, 1991.

Bowles, Paul. *The Sheltering Sky.* 1949. New York: Vintage International, 1990.

Bibliography

Brodersen, Momme. *Walter Benjamin: A Biography*. Trans. Malcolm R. Green and Ingrida Ligers. New York: Verso, 1997.

Burke, Edmund. *A Philosophical Enquiry into the Origin of Our Ideas of the Sublime and Beautiful*. Ed. J. T. Boulton. London: Routledge and Kegan Paul, 1958.

Byron, Thomas. *The Heart of Awareness: A Translation of the Ashtavakra Gita*. Boston: Shambhala, 1990.

Camus, Albert. *American Journals*. Trans. Hugh Levick. New York: Paragon House, 1987.

Camus, Albert. *The Fall*. 1956. Trans. Justin O'Brien. New York: Vintage Books, 1991.

Camus, Albert. *The Myth of Sisyphus and Other Essays*. 1955. Trans. Justin O'Brien. New York: Alfred A. Knopf, 1991.

Camus, Albert. *The Stranger*. 1946. Trans. Matthew Ward. New York: Alfred A. Knopf, 1993.

Chamberlain, Lesley. *Nietzsche in Turin: An Intimate Biography*. New York: Picador, 1996.

Cioran, E. M. *Tears and Saints*. Trans. Ilinca Zarifopol-Johnston. Chicago: University of Chicago Press, 1995.

Cleary, Thomas, ed. and trans. *Zen Essences: The Science of Freedom*. Boston: Shambhala, 1989.

Cronin, Anthony. *Samuel Beckett: The Last Modernist*. New York: HarperCollins, 1996.

Delano, Jack. *Photographic Memories*. Washington, D.C.: Smithsonian Institution Press, 1997.

Dyer, Geoff. *Out of Sheer Rage: Wrestling with D. H. Lawrence*. New York: North Point Press, 1997.

Easwaran, Eknath, trans. *The Bhagavad Gita*. Petaluma, Calif.: Nilgiri Press, 1985.

Easwaran, Eknath, trans. *The Upanishads*. Petaluma, Calif.: Nilgiri Press, 1987.

Eliot, T. S. *The Complete Poems and Plays*. London: Faber and Faber, 1969.

Emerson, Ralph Waldo. "Nature." *The Selected Writings of Ralph Waldo Emerson*. Ed. Brooks Atkinson. 3–39. New York: Random House, 1968.

Flanagan, John T. "Thoreau in Minnesota." *Minnesota History* 16 (March 1935): 35–46.

Garland, Hamlin. *Back-Trailers from the Middle Border*. New York: Macmillan, 1928.

Garland, Hamlin. *A Son of the Middle Border*. 1917. Lincoln: University of Nebraska Press, 1979.

Ginsberg, Allen. *Kaddish and Other Poems, 1958–1960*. San Francisco: City Lights Books, 1961.

Ginsberg, Allen. *Snapshot Poetics*. San Francisco: Chronicle Books, 1993.

Hammarskjöld, Dag. *Markings*. Trans. Leif Sjöberg and W. H. Auden. New York: Alfred A. Knopf, 1964.

Bibliography

Hanh, Thich Nhat. *Being Peace.* Berkeley: Parallax Press, 1987.

Herbert, Zbigniew. *Still Life with Bridle.* New York: Ecco Press, 1991.

Iyer, Pico. *Video Night in Kathmandu.* New York: Alfred A. Knopf, 1988.

Joyce, James. "The Dead." *Dubliners.* 175–223. New York: Viking Penguin, 1976.

Kant, Immanuel. *Critique of Judgement.* 1790. New York: Hafner Press, 1951.

Kierkegaard, Søren. *The Diary of Søren Kierkegaard.* Ed. Peter P. Rohde. New York: Philosophical Library, 1960.

Koerner, Joseph Leo. *Caspar David Friedrich and the Subject of Landscape.* New Haven: Yale University Press, 1990.

Kundera, Milan. *Testaments Betrayed.* New York: HarperCollins, 1995.

Lao-Tzu. *Tao Te Ching.* Trans. Stephen Mitchell. New York: Harper & Row, 1988.

Lawrence, D. H. *Mornings in Mexico.* 1927. Salt Lake City: Gibbs M. Smith, 1982.

Leopold, Aldo. *A Sand County Almanac.* 1949. New York: Oxford University Press, 1966.

Lindbergh, Charles A. *The Spirit of St. Louis.* New York: Charles Scribner's Sons, 1953.

Li Po. *The Selected Poems of Li Po.* Trans. David Hinton. New York: New Directions, 1996.

Logsdon, Gene. *The Contrary Farmer.* White River Junction, Vt.: Chelsea Green Publishing Co., 1994.

Lowenthal, Anne W., ed. *The Object as Subject: Studies in the Interpretation of Still Life.* Princeton: Princeton University Press, 1996.

Matthiessen, Peter. *The Snow Leopard.* New York: Viking Press, 1978.

Moffett, Charles, Eliza E. Rathbone, Katherine Rothkopf, and Joel Isaacson. *Impressionists in Winter: Effets de Neige.* Washington, D.C.: The Phillips Collection, 1998.

Nin, Anaïs. *The Diary of Anaïs Nin.* Vol. 3, *1939–1944.* Ed. Gunther Stuhlmann. New York: Harcourt Brace, 1969.

Oliver, Mary. *Dream Work.* Boston: Atlantic Monthly Press, 1986.

Paine, Jeffery. *Father India: How Encounters with an Ancient Culture Transformed the West.* New York: HarperCollins, 1998.

Pepys, Samuel. *The Diary of Samuel Pepys.* Ed. Robert Latham and William Matthews. New York: HarperCollins, 1995.

Pushkin, Alexander. *Boris Godunov.* Trans. Alfred Hayes. New York: Dutton, 1918.

Bibliography

Quinney, Richard. *For the Time Being: Ethnography of Everyday Life.* Albany: State University Press of New York, 1998.

Quinney, Richard. *Journey to a Far Place: Autobiographical Reflections.* Philadelphia: Temple University Press, 1991.

Quinney, Richard. *Providence: The Reconstruction of Social and Moral Order.* New York: Longman, 1980.

Rewald, Sabine, ed. *The Romantic Vision of Caspar David Friedrich.* New York: The Metropolitan Museum of Art, 1990.

Richardson, Robert D. *Henry Thoreau: A Life of the Mind.* Berkeley: University of California Press, 1986.

Rilke, Rainer Maria. *Letters to a Young Poet.* Trans. Stephen Mitchell. Boston: Shambhala, 1993.

Rilke, Rainer Maria. *The Selected Poetry of Rainer Maria Rilke.* Ed. and trans. Stephen Mitchell. New York: Random House, 1982.

Rotha, Paul. *Robert J. Flaherty: A Biography.* Ed. Jay Ruby. Philadelphia: University of Pennsylvania Press, 1983.

Ryōkan, *One Robe, One Bowl: The Zen Poetry of Ryōkan.* Trans. John Stevens. New York: Weatherhill, 1977.

Salter, James. *Burning the Days.* New York: Random House, 1997.

Sebald, W. G. *The Rings of Saturn.* Trans. Michael Hulse. New York: New Directions Books, 1998.

Seung Sahn. *Only Don't Know.* San Francisco: Four Seasons, 1982.

Shakespeare, William. *The Sonnets and Narrative Poems.* New York: Alfred A. Knopf, 1992.

Siamanto. *Bloody News from My Friend.* Trans. Peter Balakian and Nevart Yaghlian. Detroit: Wayne State University Press, 1996.

Simenon, Georges. *The Man with the Little Dog.* Trans. Jean Stewart. New York: Harcourt Brace Jovanovich, 1965.

Soames, Sally. *Writers.* San Francisco: Chronicle Books, 1995.

Sontag, Susan. *On Photography.* New York: Farrar, Straus & Giroux, 1977.

Sudek, Josef. *Josef Sudek, Poet of Prague: A Photographer's Life.* New York: Aperture, 1990.

Tanner, Michael. *Nietzsche.* New York: Oxford University Press, 1994.

Thoreau, Henry D. *The Correspondence of Henry David Thoreau.* Ed. Walter Harding and Carl Bode. New York: New York University Press, 1958.

Bibliography

Thoreau, Henry D. *The Journal of Henry D. Thoreau.* Vol. 14. Ed. Bradford Torrey and Francis H. Allen. Boston: Houghton Mifflin, 1949.

Thoreau, Henry D. *Walden.* Ed. J. Lyndon Shanley. Princeton: Princeton University Press, 1973.

Thornton, Dora. *The Scholar in His Study: Ownership and Experience in Renaissance Italy.* New Haven: Yale University Press, 1997.

Thurman, Robert. *Inner Revolution: Life, Liberty, and the Pursuit of Real Happiness.* New York: Riverhead Books, 1998.

Twitchell, James B. *Romantic Horizons: Aspects of the Sublime in English Poetry and Painting, 1770– 1850.* Columbia: University of Missouri Press, 1983.

Vansittart, Peter. *Paths from a White Horse: A Writer's Memoir.* London: Quartet Books, 1985.

Wang Wei. *Laughing Lost in the Mountains: Poems of Wang Wei.* Trans. Tony Barnstone, Willis Barnstone, and Xu Haixin. Hanover, N.H.: University Press of New England, 1991.

Whitfield, Sarah. *Bonnard.* New York: Harry Abrams, 1998.

Wieseltier, Leon. *Kaddish.* New York: Alfred A. Knopf, 1998.

Wittgenstein, Ludwig. *Tractatus Logico-Philosophicus.* Trans. C. K. Ogden. London: Routledge and Kegan Paul, 1981.

Wolfe, Linnie Marsh. *Son of the Wilderness: The Life of John Muir.* 1945. Madison: University of Wisconsin Press, 1978.

Wordsworth, William. *The Poems of William Wordsworth.* Ed. Jonathan Wordsworth. Cambridge, U.K.: University Printing House, 1973.